POTTERY TECHNIQUES
on and off the wheel

Graham Bagg

VNR VAN NOSTRAND REINHOLD COMPANY
New York Cincinnati Toronto London Melbourne

Van Nostrand Reinhold Company Regional Offices:
New York Cincinnati Chicago Millbrae Dallas

Van Nostrand Reinhold Company International Offices:
London Toronto Melbourne

Library of Congress Catalog Card Number 73-16698
ISBN 0 442 30023 9

Designed by Jerzy Karo
Photographs by Paddy Aiken A.R.P.S.

This book is filmset in Ehrhardt and *printed*
in Great Britain by BAS Printers Limited,
Wallop, Hampshire

Published by Van Nostrand Reinhold Company Inc.,
450 West 33rd Street, New York, N.Y. 10001
and Van Nostrand Reinhold Company Ltd.,
Egginton House, 25–28 Buckingham Gate,
London SW1E 6LQ

16 15 14 13 12 11 10 9 8 7 6 5 4 3 2 1

Library of Congress Cataloging in Publication Data

Bagg, Graham W
Pottery techniques on and off the wheel.
1. Pottery craft. I. Title
TT920.B33   738.1   73-16698
ISBN 0-442-30023-9

Contents

Introduction

The fascination of pottery lies in its endless variety of form and decoration. It is therefore important that, at an early stage, the pottery student should become familiar with as many techniques as possible so that they can be incorporated into individual creative work. For this reason, each assignment deals with some new aspect of making and decorating, to enable the student to build up a good background of basic craft knowledge. It has been assumed that the majority of schools and many home potters will have access only to kilns firing up to 1100°C., and it is with this in mind that techniques for stoneware and porcelain, which require higher temperatures, have not been included.

Each assignment is made up of two sections, one on the wheel and the other off the wheel, so that the course may be followed with or without the use of a potter's wheel. Both parts of each assignment, on and off the wheel, are considered to make equal demands on the student. This arrangement should meet the needs of varying school schemes and craft facilities. My own method of teaching employs on-the-wheel and off-the-wheel activities. Each child is allocated an equal amount of instruction at the wheel, and, for the remainder of the time, makes pieces by hand off the wheel, and decorates pieces already thrown. This method of working solves many organisational problems. The book is intended also to meet the needs of other pottery students seeking guidance in their study of the craft.

Considerable attention has been given to the question of design. This, it is hoped, will tie up with present-day thinking on craft education, which aims to exploit its intellectual and problem-solving aspects as well as the straightforward imparting of skills. The solution offered to each design problem is only one of many.

Any breaking down of artificial barriers between one branch of knowledge and another is to be encouraged. For this reason the way has been pointed, whenever relevant, towards that forging of links between pottery and allied crafts which plays such an important part in the development of the sensitive craftsman.

Acknowledgements

My grateful thanks are due to my wife, Mary Bagg, for all the help she has afforded me in the practical preparation of many of the off-the-wheel pieces illustrated, and especially for the excellent examples of ball and roll figurines which illustrate Assignments 6 and 7, and the pectoral in Assignment 18.

I should also like to thank Mrs Aiken for all the trouble she has taken with the photographs; the young potters of the Norton Knatchbull School, Ashford, for their co-operation; and the staff of Van Nostrand Reinhold Co. for their encouragement and untiring readiness to give me every assistance throughout the preparation of the book.

Basic Pottery Techniques

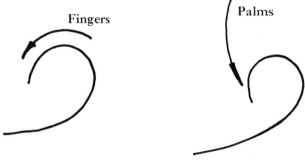

Fig. 1. Kneading.

IN POTTERY, AS IN many other crafts, there are certain basic techniques which are constantly being used. It is necessary to learn how to do these well, and this will only be achieved through continual practice. This section describes these techniques fully, and can be referred to while working through the assignments.

CLAY

Preparation

Clay is not always ready for immediate use. Even when it arrives from the supplier, it may contain mixed hard and soft clay, or different types of clay, insufficiently mixed. The clay must therefore be further mixed by the potter until it is all of the same consistency. Clay must also be free from air pockets, which appear as small blisters or holes. If present during firing they tend to expand, and crack or shatter the work; and, when throwing clay, they can cause considerable annoyance.

There are two traditional ways of making clay even and free from air. They are kneading and wedging. Both operations should be done on a well-braced wedging slab, which can be made of wood, concrete, or plaster. Kneading is perhaps more difficult than wedging, especially for someone of small build, and with small hands.

Starting with a mass of clay in a block shape, pull over the back edge with both sets of fingers, and at the crest push it down and back under itself with the palms of the hands. Give the clay a regular quarter turn, and repeat the action rhythmically for as long as necessary, until the clay seems usable.

To wedge clay, slap it with cupped hands until it becomes a solid mass with a domed top. Make a cut about two-thirds of the way down the lump with a cheese wire. Pick up the domed portion in both hands, invert it, and raising both hands above your head bring it down smartly on to the remaining third still lying on the wedging slab. The force of the impact bursts some of the air bubbles. Peel off the lump, turn it through 90 degrees, slap it into shape, and repeat the process. Peel the lump off, and this time turn it up on end to repeat the action once more. Wedge the clay as many times as necessary, until the wire-cut section reveals an even texture, and no blisters or holes.

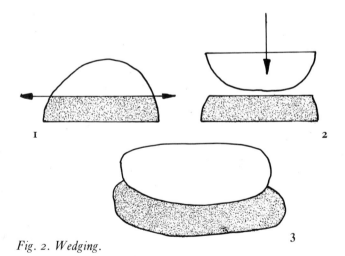

Fig. 2. Wedging.

Many pottery workshops have a small pug-mill, which is a machine used to re-condition the mixture of

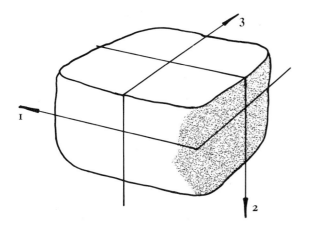

Fig. 3. *The three planes along which clay is cut during wedging.*

Fig. 4. *Luting with a modelling tool.*

dry clay and slop which accumulates when making pottery. However it is important to remember that clay pugged in the mill will not necessarily be air-free and in a fit state for use. A pug-mill is potentially a dangerous machine, and should be used with care.

Luting

Every craft has its own typical method of fixing. The potter is lucky, for the only glue he needs is liquid clay in the form of slip. When it is necessary to join leather-hard pieces of clay, for example when fixing a handle to a jug, generously cover with slip both areas which will come into contact, and then press them firmly together until the surplus slip squelches out. There will now be no air trapped in the joint.

This is the correct but narrow meaning of 'luting', and the phrase 'lute and model' occurs frequently at the end of the assignments in this book. Modelling involves pushing some clay from each piece over into the other piece, and then re-modelling the joint to the original shape. This creates a weld between the two pieces, which will remain during firing. The term 'stitching' is sometimes used for this process, since the

lines left by the modelling tool resemble a piece of needlework.

However in pottery the term 'luting' is often extended to cover both the slipping and modelling processes. It should always be remembered that sticking pieces of leather-hard clay together with slip is rarely sufficient, as the parts tend to open up as they dry, and the joint should be modelled as well.

Rolls of clay

Making clay into rolls is not quite as easy as it appears, and is a skill which will gradually be acquired. The problem is to keep the roll circular in cross-section while it is being made thinner. It will tend to become first an oval, and then a flat form. Remember that the circumference of a large roll is considerable, and to roll it only a short distance to and fro means that only part of it is being manipulated – the result will be a flat section. The secret lies in rolling the clay backwards and forwards over a distance roughly equivalent to its circumference. The roll is stretched by moving the fingers gradually outwards while rolling.

Start with a roughly modelled roll of clay, and roll it on a sheet of cartridge paper until it has thinned down

3

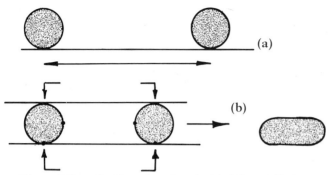

Fig. 5. Effect of rolling clay along its (a) full, and (b) less than full circumference.

to an acceptable diameter. If the roll becomes too long for the job in hand, before it has become thin enough, cut off the surplus and continue rolling.

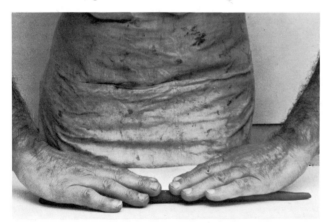

Fig. 6. Rolling clay. Note the position of the fingers.

Wad-box

Anyone doing pottery who also has some knowledge of metalwork may be interested in making a wad-box. This resembles a large grease gun or icing syringe: the container is filled with clay, which is then extruded through a die by means of a thread-controlled plunger, so forming a continuous roll or coil. By changing the die, rolls of any cross-section can be produced.

Fig. 7. Wad-box on a stand. Note the set of dies for extruding clay of different sections.

Slabs of clay

From time to time the potter needs to make flat, even slabs of clay. Use a pair of wooden slats as thick as the clay slabs are required to be. With the palms of the hands, roughly flatten out a lump of clay on a sheet of cartridge paper, and place the slats one on either side. Roll out the clay with a wooden rolling-pin, until no further rolling is possible and the rolling-pin is touching both slats. Slabs of whatever shape and size required can be cut from this with a damp knife.

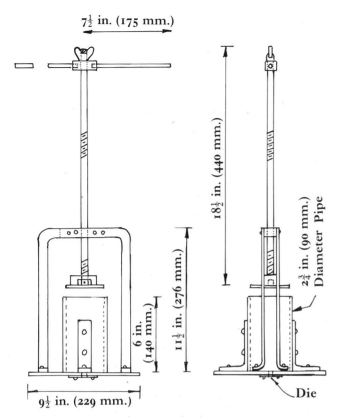

Fig. 8. Working diagram for a home-made wad-box.

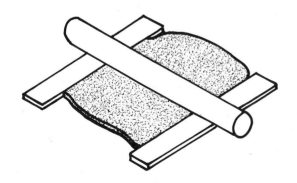

Fig. 9. Rolling a clay slab of even thickness.

Slip

Ordinary clay slip can be made by pinching clay into small pieces with the fingers, dropping these pieces into a bowl or bucket, and covering them with water. Leave the clay to disintegrate for several days, and then churn the slurry with your hand until it has the consistency of thin cream (if it is too thick, add extra water). Push this through a 60's to 80's lawn into a bucket, and cover it to prevent the slip from drying out.

DECORATION

Banding-wheel

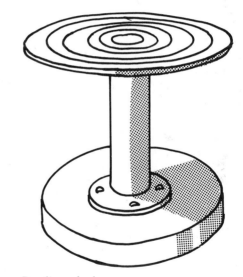

Fig. 10. Banding-wheel.

This resembles a miniature potter's wheel, and is spun by hand. It is invaluable when decorating; if the pot is centred on it, concentric bands of colour can be spun, or large areas evenly covered with a layer of slip. Spin it, like the potter's wheel, in an anti-clockwise direction, and hold the brush at an angle to the side of the pot.

5

Mixing colours for painting

Use a sheet of glass and a palette knife, and do not be afraid of pushing the knife blade hard down on the glass when grinding. Take all the powered colour and grind it with a small quantity of the medium; grind this, in turn, with the remainder of the medium. This ensures even dispersal.

Remember that the grinding process is continually sharpening the palette knife, and care must be taken when cleaning it.

Fig. 11. Grinding colour with a palette knife on a glass slab.

MOULDED POTTERY

Casting-slip

When clay is cast in a plaster mould, special deflocculated casting-slip must be prepared. Ordinary slip contains far too much water, takes a long time to dry, and would quickly make the moulds wet.

It will help you co-ordinate the craft of pottery with its scientific basis if you know that particles of clay are all negatively charged and therefore repel each other. The addition of small quantities of certain positively charged alkaline substances creates attraction, and breaks the bond between the particles. The process is known as deflocculation. The alkalis normally used are sodium carbonate (soda ash) and sodium silicate (isinglass).

Each type of clay requires a different deflocculating recipe. The clay supplier will usually tell you what are the optimum quantities of alkali and water for a particular clay. A typical recipe for a white earthenware is as follows.

Powdered clay	5 lb. (2.3 kg.)
Sodium silicate $75^{\circ T}$	$\frac{1}{2}$ oz. (11 g.)
Sodium carbonate	$\frac{1}{2}$ oz. (11 g.)
Water	35 fl. oz. (1 litre)

Different quantities of water are of course required for a plastic clay. The descriptive number that follows sodium silicate in the recipe gives a measure of its specific gravity in degrees Twaddell, where actual specific gravity equals degrees Twaddell divided by 200. Both $75^{\circ T}$ and $140^{\circ T}$ sodium silicate are available.

Casting-slip is prepared as follows.

(1) Weigh out a known quantity of plastic or powdered clay. If using plastic clay, break it up as if making ordinary slip.

(2) Weigh out the alkalis, and dissolve them in the very small quantity of hot water in the recipe.

(3) Pour the solution over the clay, cover the container with a polythene sheet, tie down, and leave the chemicals to work for 12–24 hours.

(4) Beat up the mixture with a flat stick. The more it is beaten up, the easier it will be to sieve.

(5) Push this rough slip through an 80's lawn, and store it under a polythene cover until required.

It is easy to distinguish casting-slip from ordinary slip, because when left to stand, it is jelly-like, and when stirred, it has a distinctive mottled surface.

Mixing plaster

Plaster for use in mould-making must be of the correct strength and porosity. If too hard, it will not adequately absorb the moisture from the casting-slip. The correct proportion is $2\frac{3}{4}$ lb. (1.3 kg.) to every 40 fl. oz. (1.1 litres) of water.

The procedure for mixing plaster is as follows.
(1) Fill a bucket with the correct amount of water, and weigh out the plaster.
(2) Sift the plaster into the water, but on no account stir it as this causes lumpiness. When all the plaster has been tipped in, there should be a little hill above the surface of the water. Allow the plaster to slake and take up water slowly.
(3) When all the plaster has dispersed, and no more air bubbles are being released from the dry particles, agitate the mixture from the bottom of the bowl, with the hand held palm-upwards.

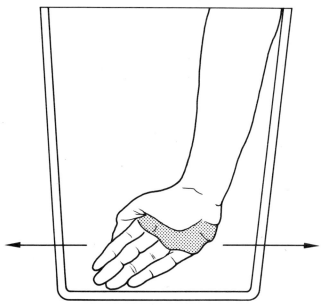

Fig. 12. Stirring plaster in a bucket.

(4) Watch the contents carefully, as setting often occurs quite rapidly. Draw your finger over the surface of the plaster: if this action leaves a small wake, setting has begun and the plaster must be poured immediately. Pouring is quite impossible if delayed too long.

Soap-size

This is the resist agent which is used to prevent one plaster surface from adhering to another. It is prepared as follows.
(1) Dissolve a lump of soft soap (*sapo mollis*) about the size of a hen's egg in 8 fl. oz. (0.2 litres) of hot water. The process is speeded up if the water is kept hot in a saucepan over heat.
(2) When completely dissolved, add one or two drops of olive oil.
(3) Allow the solution to cool, and then store it in a screw-top bottle.

A plaster surface is made non-porous as follows.
(1) Pour on a little of the soap-size and brush it well over the surface, whipping up a good lather. An old shaving brush is ideal.
(2) Wash the surface thoroughly under running water, and sponge it dry.
(3) Repeat.
(4) Lather the surface for the third time, but do not wash it. Instead, wring out the sponge and remove any remaining lather with it.

The treated surface should look like a piece of old ivory, and resist any water dropped on it.

GENERAL

Sieving

This is a common operation in pottery. Glazes and liquidised clays must be sieved to ensure proper mixing, to eliminate lumps, and to eradicate any foreign matter. The sieves used are called lawns, and are made of finely woven phosphor bronze, stretched tightly across a wooden hoop. Lawns are graded from 5's to 300's, according to the number of apertures per linear inch. The most convenient sizes for general pottery work are 80's for sieving slips, and 120's for sieving glazes.

To sieve material, place a couple of wooden slats across a bucket or bowl, just far enough apart for the edge of the lawn to rest on them, and then push the

Fig. 13. Bucket set up for sieving.

material through with a lawn brush. Remember that the small apertures in the gauze soon block up if not kept clean, so always wash the lawn well as soon as it is finished with.

Assignment 1 – on the Wheel

Cylindrical Mug

IT IS NOT EASY TO make a pot on the wheel, but it is very exciting. You will enjoy the feeling of clay alive in your hands, and will quickly gain confidence.

As in many other crafts, you will have to learn the correct hand movements, evolved from the experience of generations of craftsmen. No doubt your instructor will demonstrate how to throw a simple pot. Watch carefully, see where he places his hands and arms, notice the speed of his movements and how he stands at the wheel. Try to make a mental picture of each movement, so that you can use your own hands on the wheel in the same way.

Always stand tightly against the wheel and crouch over it, bending your back. Pots cannot be made by remote control! Your arms and hands must be as stable as possible. This makes for a true pot, and is vital when centring the clay. Try not to be too tensed, though, as a certain controlled flexibility is called for. Keep your arms to your sides with elbows well back, so that there is little play between the clay and your arm. This is similar to wood turning, where the chisel is held as near the work as possible. Keep the hands and the clay wet; working dry will create friction and cause trouble. The hands must never be still on the clay. If you remain in one position, the hands adopt the rôle of a cutter, and part of the clay will separate from the rest. The hands must always work in unison: it is fatal, for instance, to have the left hand inside the bottom of the pot while the right hand is dealing with the outside centre.

It is a good idea to start by aiming to throw a simple cylindrical mug, without making any attempt to shape it.

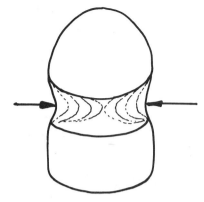

Fig. 14. Effect of holding the hands in one position when throwing.

WORK SEQUENCE

(1) Take a piece of wedged clay about 1 lb. (454 g.) in weight and, using cupped hands, pat it into a ball as if making a snowball.

(2) Start the wheel and damp it with a squeezed-out sponge. Do not use a wet sponge, as clay will not adhere to a wet wheel.

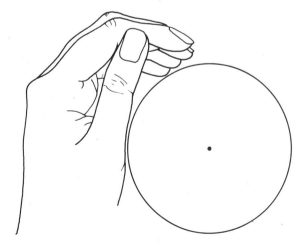

Fig. 15. 'Pocketing the bull's eye' with the left hand.

(3) Cup the left hand and place it lightly on the wheel, as if holding the clay ball. This is known as 'pocketing the bull's eye', and will help you throw the clay in the right place. Now hold the ball in the right hand and throw it smartly on to the wheel, aiming to hit the centre from directly above. This will fasten the clay firmly to the wheel. Once the ball has been thrown, take your hands away and see how it is spinning. If it is very eccentric, stop the wheel, and with both hands round the ball pull it nearer to the centre. This requires quite a strong pull and will prove just how firmly the ball is attached to the wheel.

(4) A symmetrical cylinder cannot be made from a ball of clay which is not running perfectly true. The first step, therefore, is to centre the clay. Stand right against the wheel, and rest the palms of your hands on the clay, with the little fingers resting on the moving wheel, in such a way that you can bring pressure to bear across the diameter of the clay. Pressure exerted elsewhere not only wastes effort, but tends to push the clay away from the centre.

Wet the clay and your hands; now press inwards with both hands, at the same time raising them gradually upwards to the top of the clay. You will feel bumps where the clay is bulging, but try not to let your hands and arms be moved by them. Repeat this two or three times. Inspection of the top of the clay will show you

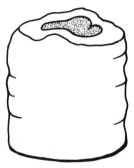

Fig. 17. *Effect of squeezing an irregular clay mass without coning.*

that the irregularities are being brought to the top. The top in itself will still be far from level. This can be rectified by the process known as coning. The next time you bring your hands up the side of the clay, overlap your fingers, one over the other, making your hands 'nozzle' progressively smaller. At the end of this move-

Fig. 16. *Centring. Note the position of the hands.*

Fig. 18. *Clay shape after the first coning.*

ment you will see that the clay is taking the shape of an inverted ice-cream cone. Pointing the clay removes the irregularity at the top, and since the diameter gets gradually smaller it is easier to push the bulges to the centre. Remember that the smaller the diameter, the less pressure will be required. As you get used to this process, keep your hands on the clay and return from the top of the cone to the bottom, reversing the 'nozzle' action so that a continuous centring action is maintained. Keep your hands and the clay wet the whole time.

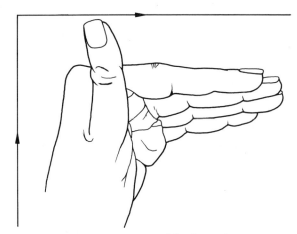

Fig. 20. Position of the left hand for depressing.

Take your hand away, and you will see that a mushroom shape has been made on top of the cone.

Fig. 19. Coning.

Fig. 21. The mushroom formed when depressing with the left hand only.

(5) Coning helps to centre the clay, but a cone is not a good shape from which to form a pot. You must now try to bring the clay back to a hump shape on the wheel. This is called depressing. Bend your left hand at the knuckles, so that the fingers form a right angle with the palm; press the thumb tightly against the first finger, and bend the top thumb joint as far back towards the wrist as possible. This forms a fleshy cushion at the base of the thumb. Place this cushion on top of the clay cone so that your fingers point obliquely down its side, and, keeping your arm rigid, push down a little.

The right hand must now resolve the mushroom by inward pressure into the main mass of clay, and so form a dome shape. Place your left hand as it was before, but this time put the fingers of your right hand on those of your left, and your right thumb on your left thumb. Then push slowly down with your left hand, and hard towards the centre with your right hand. A dome will automatically be produced, provided you do not move your left hand.

Fig. 22. Depressing.

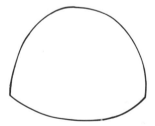

Fig. 23. Shape of the clay after depressing correctly with both hands.

The clay should now be central and running true. If it is still eccentric, repeat the coning and depressing processes as many times as necessary.

Fig. 24. Position of the hands at the end of the depressing movement ; the clay is fully centred.

(6) Once the clay is centred, it can be hollowed. Put both hands round the clay dome and find the centre with your right thumb. Press your thumb down into the clay without moving your hands away. (If you just use your free thumb, the hole you make will be far from central.) Do not, of course, press completely through to the wheel, but leave about $\frac{3}{8}$ in. (10 mm.) of clay to form the bottom of the clay cylinder.

Fig. 25. Making the first opening in the clay mass.

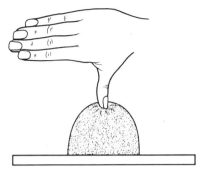

Fig. 26. Incorrect position for making the first opening in the mass.

(7) This first entry hole must be widened to the desired internal size of the cylinder. Lean right over the wheel. Grip your left wrist with your right finger tips, put your left hand round the clay, and let your right thumb touch the bottom of the entry hole. Press towards yourself with the fleshy pad at the top of your right thumb, until you have widened the entry to the desired size.

Fig. 27. Making the second opening in the clay mass.

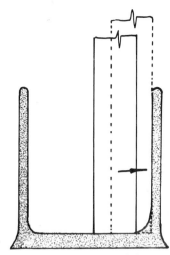

Fig. 28. Squaring the inner corners of the mug with a ruler.

(8) Your thumb is curved, so the bottom corners of the inside will naturally also be curved. With all your finger tips to the front and your two thumbs behind, grip a short ruler vertically, brace your wrists against your body, rest the end of the ruler on the right side of the base centre, and gradually move it to the right until the side of the ruler is in contact with the inside clay wall. This will give the mug a good clean inside corner.

(9) The clay wall, which is at this stage very short and thick, must now be raised and thinned. Bend the first finger of the right hand at the second knuckle, and tuck the remaining fingers tightly into the palm. Push the thumb as far away from the first finger as possible, and arch the whole hand so that you can touch the wheel with the knuckle of the first finger and your thumb, which should be as far from each other as possible. Hold your hand like this on the wheel until you get used to the thrust and are not tempted to go round with the motion of the wheel. Then bring both knuckle and thumb against the clay, so that the side of your first finger rests vertically against the side of the clay wall. Place the fingers of your left hand inside the pot, and hook the thumb over the top of the wall, bringing it

13

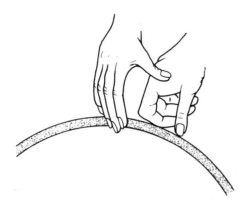

Fig. 29. Position of the fingers when raising the wall.

Fig. 30. Raising the clay wall.

to rest on the back of your right hand. Now bring both hands slowly up the side of the clay in unison until the clay is lost at the top. This will give practice in working both hands together.

When you feel confident, instead of just moving the hands up the clay, press evenly and gently between them to force the clay wall upwards. Watch carefully what is happening: the diameter should remain constant – if it begins to widen, the left hand is pressing too hard, and vice versa. Maintain an even pressure – uneven pressure will produce a wobbly cylinder with walls of uneven thickness. Reduce pressure evenly at the top, so that the clay glides easily out of your fingers. Repeat this movement as often as necessary until the wall is of an acceptable thickness.

If the top is uneven by this time, it can be trued with a needle point or compass. Let the clay wall run loosely between the first finger tip and thumb of your left hand. Hold the needle in your right hand and rest it on your left thumb so that it meets the clay wall at the right height. Gradually feed the needle into the clay until the irregular portion is completely free and can be lifted away.

Fig. 31. Needle or pricker.

14

Fig. 32. *Trimming the top edge with a needle.*

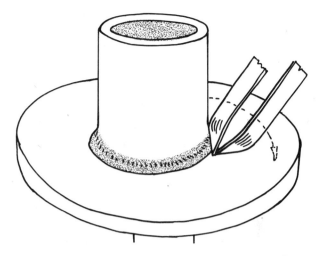

Fig. 34. *Trimming the side of a thrown pot with the side tool.*

Because of the natural shape of the knuckle, the outside of the mug will be curved in the same way as the inside was curved by the thumb, and where the outside meets the wheel it must be cleaned to a sharper angle.

Fig. 33. *Side tool.*

A side tool, which has two sharpened edges meeting at a point, is used for this. Hold the tool firmly, as shown in Fig. 34, and cut down the excess fillet of clay; pivot the tool at its point, and the other edge will then be in position to clean the clay from the wheel.

(10) Flood the wheel with water, hold a cutting wire taut and flat on the wheel with both hands, and push it smartly underneath the pot. This brings water underneath the clay, and frees it so that when the mug is pressed gently at the bottom with the finger tips of the right hand, it slides to the edge. Damp a small board, and hold it level with the wheel so that you can slide the mug straight on to it. With more experience you will be able to slide it on to the fingers of your left hand and carry it to a board.

(11) Put the mug aside to dry until it is leather-hard and can be handled safely.

(12) The mug will be rather untidy where it was cut from the wheel. It can be cleaned up by a process called turning, the potter's wheel being used as a vertical lathe.

Damp the wheel and place the mug upside down in the centre of it (an experienced potter will tap it to the centre). Many wheels have concentric rings engraved on them, which enable the potter to position the mug centrally without too much difficulty. If you have a plain wheel, spin a few lines on it with a pencil. When the mug is in position, fix it to the wheel in three places with a little clay. Take a flat-sided turning tool, support the spinning mug with your left hand, and true the bottom edge of the mug with the tool. Rest the left thumb against the tool to keep it steady. Turn the tool on its side and, working from the centre outwards, flatten the bottom.

A well-finished pot also has a foot turned into the base. Firstly, this makes the pot lighter. Secondly,

Fig. 35. Turning a foot.

during firing the bottom of a pot sometimes bulges and it becomes unstable. If the piece has a foot, however, a bulge makes little difference to its level standing. Thirdly, if the pot is to be glaze-fired without using a stilt, it must have a glaze-free foot to stand on in the kiln.

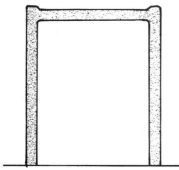

Fig. 36. Foot turned on the mug.

Turn the base again from the centre, but stop about $\frac{3}{16}$ in. (5 mm.) from the edge. Repeat this several times until a small rim is formed at the outer edge. Lastly, use the turning tool to remove the sharp edges from either side of the rim. Take the mug off the wheel, and

clean up any remaining fixing clay.

(13) The mug is now made, but it also needs a simple handle. Roll out between slats a piece of clay $\frac{3}{16}$ in. (5 mm.) thick, and from it cut a strip about $\frac{5}{8}$ in. (15 mm.) wide and 4 in. (100 mm.) long. Turn this on edge on a paper-covered board and coax it into a suitable curve to fit the mug. Hold the mug over it to check for size, and then put the handle aside to dry, until both mug and handle are leather-hard.

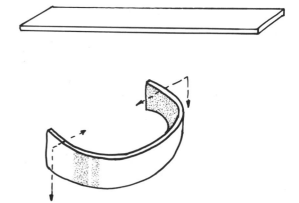

Fig. 37. Making a flat handle.

(14) To fit the handle exactly to the mug, pare it with a knife, coat the ends and the corresponding mug positions with slip, and press them together, supporting the inside with the fingers; finally, lute them together with a modelling tool. Any slight gap at the joint can be filled in with a little extra clay. Sponge the whole piece until it is clean and tidy.

DECORATION

(1) Use a soft brush to paint two 'windows' with white slip, one on the back and one on the front of the mug.
(2) Sketch a few shapes, each roughly the same size as the window, and draw some simple little motifs in them.
(3) When the slip has dried (it will cease to look shiny), scratch into it the chosen motif. Use a small modelling

Fig. 38. Pattern for a sgraffito window.

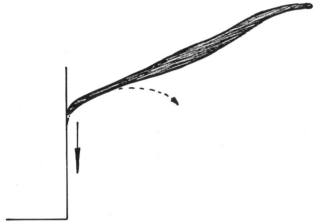

Fig. 39. Using a modelling tool for sgraffito.

tool for this, and hold it point-downwards to produce clean edges; if used on its side, the edges will be burred. Press sufficiently hard to remove the white slip completely and expose the brown clay underneath.

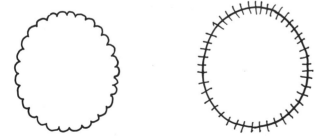

Fig. 40. Two examples showing how the window edge may be softened.

(4) The window will be enhanced by softening its outline. Some simple ways of doing this are shown in Fig. 40.

(5) Leave the mug to dry out, ready for the biscuit-fire.

(6) Finally, glaze it with a coloured transparent glaze to produce two tones – light where it covers the white slip, and dark where it covers the brown clay.

Fig. 41. Mug, before and after assembling the handle and decorating.

17

Assignment 1 – off the Wheel

Pot for Water and Paintbrushes

THIS IS A USEFUL little pot, designed to hold both water and brushes. The basic pot from which it is made is known as a thumb pot, or pinch pot.

WORK SEQUENCE AND DECORATION

(1) Take a piece of clay about 1 lb. (454 g.) in weight, and make a ball from it by patting it between cupped hands.

(2) Place the clay ball on a piece of cartridge paper about $3\frac{1}{4}$ in. (80 mm.) square, resting on a flat table.

(3) Give it a light tap with the palm of the right hand. This will convert the spherical ball into a flat cake shape.

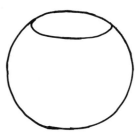

Fig. 42. Slightly flattened ball shape from which to make a thumb pot.

(4) Place your hands round the clay, find the centre of the clay mass, and then press the right thumb well down into it, leaving about $\frac{5}{8}$ in. (15 mm.) at the base.

(5) Place both thumbs into this cavity, resting the fingers conveniently over the top rim. The finger tips should be level with the thumbs, as shown in Fig. 43. Maintaining this position, move the pot (attached to the paper) through 45 degrees, at the same time giving the clay a little squeeze between the fingers and thumbs. Lift the hands and return them to the original positions, then repeat the movement. Continue in this way, and try to work rhythmically since this will keep the pot round.

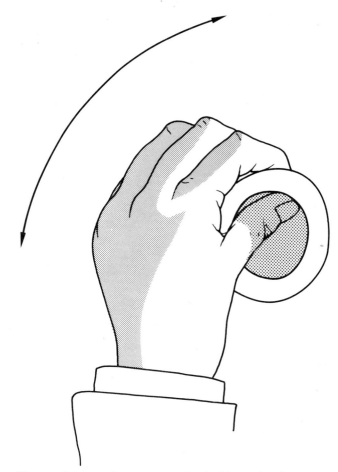

Fig. 43. One complete movement in pinching a thumb pot.

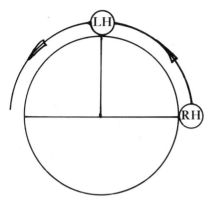

Fig. 44. Rhythmic quarter turn movement of the hands in forming a thumb pot.

Work from the bottom, and as this becomes thinned, gradually move the thumbs and fingers up the side wall to produce height. If the rim is kept thick for a while, it will prevent the pot from spreading unnecessarily. You may find it easier to shape the top portion by pressing between the finger and thumb of the right hand only, but continue to revolve the pot regularly with your left hand. Squeeze only a small portion at a time, to avoid losing the shape. If the clay begins to get dry, moisten your hands in a bowl of water. Avoid wetting the clay directly, however, as this makes a soggy, uncontrollable mess.

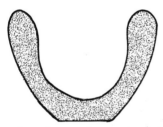

Fig. 45. Section through a partly completed thumb pot, showing top left thick to prevent spreading.

Aim at making a shape about 2¾ in. (70 mm.) in diameter at the top, and 1¾—2 in. (45—50 mm.) in

height, and try to make the walls of even thickness throughout.

(6) Squeezing will probably have made the top of the pot uneven, and it must now be levelled. Cut out a rectangle of card, and stand it on end with its side edge against the pot. Mark on the card the lowest point of

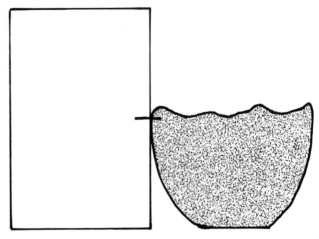

Fig. 46. Marking the level of the top.

the rim, which is the maximum height of the pot. Place the card at regular short intervals round the pot, and at each point make a mark on the clay to correspond with the mark on the card. Join these marks together with a thin line, and cut along it with a damp knife to remove the irregular top edge.

Set the pot aside to harden a little.

(7) Roll out a flat pancake of clay, between $\frac{3}{16}$ in. (5 mm.) slats. Set a pair of compasses to the radius of the outside rim of the pot, and draw a circle on the pancake of clay. Increase this radius by $\frac{7}{8}$ in. (20 mm.) and, using the same centre, draw a second circle.

(8) Cut round the line of this outer circle with a damp knife, and leave the circle to harden.

(9) When both plate and pot are leather-hard, cover the rim of the pot with slip, and also paint a ring of slip just inside the first circle. Place the pot, rim down,

19

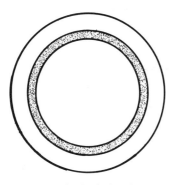

Fig. 47. Painting clay with slip before luting.

Fig. 48. Components of the watercolour pot, luted together before piercing.

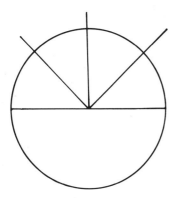

Fig. 49. Determining the position of the brush holes.

on this circle. Press the two together, and lightly model the joint on the outside.

(10) Draw on a piece of paper a circle of the same diameter as the plate. Draw the diameter and, in one of the semi-circles formed, quarter lines. Extend all these lines beyond the circumference.

Fit the plate, with pot attached, exactly over the circle; using the extended lines, transfer the quarter positions on to the clay rim. Find the centre of the rim at these points, and pierce holes with the handle of your smallest paintbrush. Turn the pot over, and press the handle through again from the other side. This will make a little burr, which should be trimmed away and sponged. Widen some of the holes with larger paint-brush handles. The handles should pass right through the holes at this stage. After firing and glazing the holes will be smaller, and the brushes will stand in them without falling through.

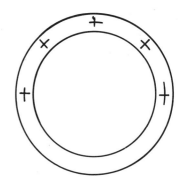

Fig. 50. Position of the brush holes.

(11) Stand the pot the right way up and, starting from the middle, cut away the plate to reveal the inside. Pare back carefully, until the cut is level with the inside pot rim. It is now possible to lute the joint between the pot and the flange from the inside – make a neat, strong job of this.

(12) Clean the whole pot with a damp sponge, and set it aside to dry out ready for the biscuit-fire.

(13) Glaze the pot with a bright-coloured opaque glaze.

Fig. 51. Components of the watercolour pot (left and centre), and the completed piece (right).

Assignment 2 –
on the Wheel
Small Vase with
Shaped Walls

IN ASSIGNMENT 1 YOU learned how to throw a cylinder of clay and how to lift the clay wall by pressing with both hands evenly, one against the other. Whenever you have the opportunity, practise this exercise to help gain confidence. The next stage up from a simple cylinder is a shaped pot.

DESIGN

Cut out some pieces of thin white card, each about 5 in. (120 mm.) square. Fold each in half, and imagine the crease line to be the centre line of a vase. On one side of this centre line, sketch a shape for the vase. It is advisable at this early stage to design in the form of a continuous line and to avoid sudden changes in diameter. Vary shape and proportions from one card to another, adding an appropriate base and top line to indicate height, and top and bottom diameter. With a pencil and set square draw a vertical line from the base to the top of the vase.

Now fold each piece of card along the centre line, with the sketched design on the outside of the fold. Cut the two thicknesses simultaneously along the drawn line, so that when the card is unfolded complete vase shapes will appear. Stand these up on the base line and examine them critically.

You will have personal preferences for one shape or another, but remember when making your choice that a good design must always take into account both the material in which it is made, and the intended function of the finished piece. Decide whether the shape you have drawn is simple and attractive, or intricate and

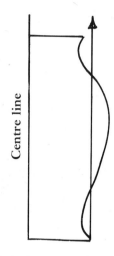

Fig. 52. Cylinder line when throwing.

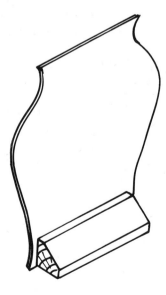

Fig. 53. Vase template held upright by a block of wood.

fussy – which is better suited to the piece you are making? Does the design have the fluid shape one expects from a plastic material, and is it an easy shape to clean? Is the mouth the right size for the kind of flower arrangement you have in mind? Will the vase be stable when full of water?

When you have chosen the shape, glue on a little block of wood at the bottom of the cut-out and stand it up on the shelf behind the potter's wheel, so that you can see it as you work.

WORK SEQUENCE

Fig. 54. Shaping the vase.

(1) Prepare a ball of clay and throw it to a cylindrical shape of the same height as the vertical line drawn on the design.

(2) Whatever shape you have drawn, the cylinder must be bulged out at some points and pressed in at others. Crouch right over the clay cylinder and take up the same position as you did for lifting the wall. Move both hands together either outwards (to bulge) or inwards (to waist), moving both hands slowly but evenly upwards in unison. During this process watch your right index finger, and observe the shape which is being produced. You will probably be cautious at first, especially if you notice that the vase tends to lose its rotundity for a time, which always happens. Complete the movement right to the top, until the clay is lost.

If the vase is not yet sufficiently shaped, repeat the movement, if necessary, several times over.

DECORATION

Either a border or windows, outlined by small rolls of clay and filled with a simple textural pattern, would be very suitable.

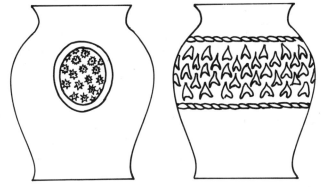

Fig. 55. Examples of impressed decoration.

(1) Make some rolls of clay $\frac{5}{16}$ in. (7—8 mm.) in section.

(2) Draw pencil guide-lines on the vase where you wish to fix the rolls. Lines for a border can be made

23

with the aid of a banding-wheel. Window lines can be drawn by cutting out a template in white card, and drawing round it.

(3) Cut the rolls to the required length.

(4) Paint the guide-lines and the backs of the rolls with slip, and press them into position on the vase without distorting their round shape. Alternatively, a good bond can be made by pressing the roll regularly with a modelling tool to simulate a rope pattern.

(5) Texture the area between the rolls with any interesting object that you can find. Some examples of textural marks are shown in Fig. 55. A pen nib, glass tubing, a comb, a table fork, a screw, and a washer are a small selection of the readily available objects that can be used.

Fig. 56. The shaped, turned vase (left), and the same vase decorated with clay rolls and impressions (right).

(6) When decoration is complete, set the vase aside to dry ready for the biscuit-fire.

(7) Apply an opaque glaze to the vase.

Assignment 2 – off the Wheel

Pebble Pot

THIS IS AN ASYMMETRICAL pot, ideal for short-stemmed flowers such as primroses and violets. As the design is an integral part of the vase, design and work sequence have not been dealt with separately.

DESIGN, WORK SEQUENCE AND DECORATION

Much can be learnt from natural objects about shape, colour, and texture. Look at some ordinary pebbles, and notice how they are all of varied shape and worn beautifully smooth. Choose one that appeals to you, and then proceed as follows.

(1) Cover the pebble with two or three layers of soft paper (orange papers or paper tissues are ideal) and fasten the loose ends with Sellotape.

(2) Wedge some clay, and cover the paper-coated pebble with a layer about $\frac{5}{16}$ in. (7 mm.) thick, modelling it with the fingers to follow the contour of the pebble. If you apply the clay in a number of separate pieces, be sure to model each new piece well to the next.

(3) Examine the pebble carefully, and draw a line round it on that plane where it would naturally divide in half.

(4) Use a damp knife to cut along this line and through the paper beneath.

(5) Now remove each 'half' from the pebble – the two parts will look rather like the halves of a chocolate Easter egg.

(6) Let these parts become leather-hard, and then remove the paper. If it is difficult to remove, leave it, since it will in any case burn away in the kiln. Cover the

cut edges generously with slip and press the two halves together, luting the joint with a modelling tool and adding any extra clay that is necessary. You now

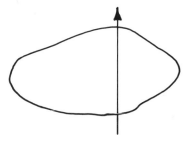

Fig. 57. Natural division line on the pebble.

Fig. 59. Stages in making a pebble pot: the pebble (foreground), the pebble covered with clay (left), the clay cut in two with the pebble removed (background), and the completed pot (right).

have a hollow clay 'pebble' of the same basic shape as the original.

(7) Study the form from all angles and move it about. Decide which way it sits naturally. The top surface of the 'pebble' is to be pierced to hold flowers – decide what this is to look like. It may be helpful to draw some chalk lines on the pebble, since these can be erased as often as necessary.

(8) When a satisfactory solution has been found, sketch on to the pot the shapes to be cut out, and pierce them with a small damp knife (a penknife is ideal).

Soften the edges with a modelling tool, and damp sponge the whole piece. Dust the pot with some fine silver sand or grog, and push these grains into the surface of the clay to create a realistic, pebble-like texture.

(9) Leave the pot to dry, ready for the biscuit-fire.
(10) Glaze the inside with an opaque glaze to make the earthenware watertight, but leave the outside unglazed in contrast.

Fig. 58. Examples of piercing to suit a pebble shape.

25

Assignment 3 –
on the Wheel

Small Milk Jug

IT IS VERY IMPORTANT to practise throwing cylinders because, as was seen in Assignment 2, a cylinder forms the basis of a number of shapes. Making a small jug will provide more practice on the same lines, for a jug is really a small vase with the addition of a lip and a handle.

DESIGN

Fig. 60. An unstable jug shape.

Consider what size the jug should be. If, for instance, it is for an early morning tea tray, it could be very small indeed. Remember that the shape of the jug must be an easy one to wash out. Think about proportions: the jug should not be too high in relation to the width of the base, or it will be unstable. It should feel well-balanced when pouring, and the position of the handle is important here. The cross-sectional size must also be considered, but it will be easier to decide on this later, when the body of the jug is complete.

Now make a number of sketches of your proposed jug. Some you will like, and some will appear ugly; others may just not do the job efficiently. Choose a sketch which looks attractive, and which fulfils all the other requirements. Draw it on card and cut it out full size.

Fig. 61. Correct (top left), and incorrect features in a jug handle.

WORK SEQUENCE

(1) Throw the body of the jug, following the same sequence of operations as for the vase in Assignment 2, but try to be a little more careful now about throwing to size. Measure the height against your full size cutout, and with a pair of callipers check on the top and bottom diameter.

Fig. 62. The first stage in making a lip.

(2) Make a 'V' shape with the first and second fingers of the left hand. Rest these two fingers vertically against the upper edge of the jug and pull the side of it between them, with an up, over and round motion of the index finger of your right hand. The final rounding movement ensures a double curve and prevents the milk dripping when poured.

Fig. 63. The second stage in making a lip.

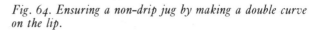

Fig. 64. Ensuring a non-drip jug by making a double curve on the lip.

(3) Cut the jug from the wheel, turn a foot on the bottom, and then put the jug aside to dry.

(4) Handles can be made in a variety of ways. Instead of making a handle from a flat piece of clay (as in Assignment 1), it will be a good idea to make one of a more traditional type.

Obtain some 17 or 18 s.w.g. galvanised iron wire, and a tapered piece of wood, metal, or bone (a nail punch is ideal).

(5) To make the tapered piece of wood into a former, fix it securely in a vice, and bend a length of wire round it at a point in the taper which will give a suitable cross-section for the handle. Pull tightly on the ends of the wire against the former, and at the same time twist the wire by moving the right hand round and under the left, and the left hand round and over the right. Repeat, changing wire ends before each movement, until about 4 in. (100 mm.) have been twisted in this way. Finish off the ends in a wire loop.

Fig. 65. Making a handle wire round a former.

27

It is useful to make several such wires of varying diameter, and build up a collection of sizes. The working loop can be modified by bending it into a flatter or more decorative cross-section with a pair of small round-nosed pliers.

(6) Shape a piece of wedged clay in the form of a small brick, and fill a small bowl with water. Trace the shape of the jug handle on to a piece of cartridge paper on a small board.

(7) Damp the wire in the bowl of water and, holding it as shown in Fig. 66, pull it vertically through the clay, taking great care not to twist it. Sometimes the clay handle so formed will pull straight out of the clay. If it remains trapped, open the clay each side with the full length of the thumbs, and lift the handle out from the top. On one side of the handle there will be a fettle line, made by the twisted wires as they were pulled through the clay.

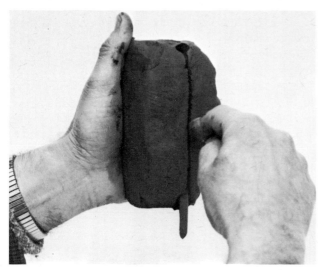

Fig. 66. Pulling a handle with a wire.

(8) Keeping the fettle line on the inside, place the handle on its side over the tracing. Coax the handle into the required shape. Ignore excess length at this stage. Hold the turned pot above it for a final check on correct curvature – looking down on both pot and handle will give an impression of how the two will fit together.

(9) Leave the newly-made handle to dry to the same degree as the pot.

(10) When ready, trim any excess off the handle with a knife, and fit the ends accurately to the shape of the jug. Cover the ends generously with slip. Find the exact corresponding points of contact on the jug, opposite the lip, and coat these with slip. Press the handle into position, supporting the inside of the jug with the left hand. Finally lute the joints thoroughly with a modelling tool. Add any necessary clay to make good the line, and clean up with a damp sponge.

DECORATION

A leather-hard pot becomes much more interesting if decorated with slip of a contrasting colour. There is little colour scope in natural clays, as most fire either brown or creamy-white, depending on the presence or absence respectively of iron oxide. It is possible to make coloured slip, however, and it can be used to decorate the completed jug.

(1) Decide how much decoration you wish to apply, and sketch your ideas. A repeat border pattern is attractive, but you must first measure the circumference of the portion of the jug to be decorated. Divide this up as necessary to accommodate the pattern and ensure that the start and finish meet up perfectly.

(2) Now mix the coloured slip. Most colours can be produced by adding between five and twenty per cent of body stain (which is in powder form) to some sieved white slip. Grind the body stain well into the slip with a muller or palette knife on a piece of glass. Blues, greens, greys, yellows, and pinks can be produced. For black, grind a little manganese dioxide with some brown slip. Contrast can be provided by using white slip in its natural state.

(3) Draw the design lightly with a pencil on the leather-hard jug. The banding-wheel will help in making the border lines.

Fig. 67. Examples of designs suitable for a painted motif or border.

(4) Damp the jug lightly with a sponge: this will roughen the surface a little and make the slip adhere well. Paint in the pattern with a watercolour brush. Clear separation of the colours can be produced by employing a sgraffito technique, and delineating the coloured areas with a modelling tool.

(5) When painting is complete, leave the jug in the damp box (overnight if possible). This will enable the painted slip, which is wetter, to adjust itself to the leather-hard pot. On no account should slip be painted on a pot which has dried beyond the leather-hard stage.

(6) Leave the jug to dry, ready for the biscuit-fire.

(7) Use a clear transparent glaze on the jug.

Fig. 68. Jug before final assembly (left), and decorated with coloured slip ready for biscuit-firing (right).

Assignment 3 – off the Wheel

Modelled Prehistoric Animal

Visit a Natural History Museum and look at any reconstructed models of prehistoric animals. If this is not possible, go to your school or local public library and browse through some books dealing with life in prehistoric times.

DESIGN

Choose an animal which seems to have an interesting shape, and try to make a mental picture of its nature. Decide whether it is basically a slimy seal-like creature, or a scaly dragon-like creature with large claws. Examine its form – is it long and sleek and smooth, or squat and huge? Now paint or draw two large silhouettes. One should show the side view of the animal, and the other how it would appear from above.

Before starting to model, pause for a while to consider the nature and behaviour of clay. The modelling or throwing body you will use is beautifully plastic, and is therefore very easy to pull and squeeze into clean flowing shapes. This means, firstly, that most of the animal can be formed from one piece of clay; secondly, thin, unsupported pieces of clay can be very vulnerable and easily broken off, so it is wise to manipulate the form of the animal a little, to avoid such danger spots.

Remember that small pieces of clay dry out much more rapidly than thicker ones, so during the course of modelling the animal it may be necessary to keep the thinner parts damp, to avoid premature drying and cracking.

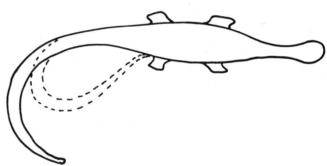

Fig. 70. Manipulating form to suit the nature of clay.

WORK SEQUENCE

(1) Start with a generous lump of clay – squeeze and pull it out slowly with the fingers until it has taken on a simple shape roughly corresponding to the profile of your animal. Pay special attention to making a good, smooth link-up between the legs and body underneath.

If the clay is particularly soft it may be necessary to support some parts until they have dried a little.

Fig. 69. Front and plan silhouette of animal.

Fig. 71. *The initial solid model of the basic form* (left), *and the two halves hollowed after cutting, ready for re-joining* (right).

(2) Examine your modelling from above, and now gently shape it to resemble the top view in your drawing. At this stage ignore detail and concentrate only on line and bulk form. Set the piece aside to harden until it can be safely handled.

(3) It is not advisable to fire a modelled figure solid, as it would be liable to crack and would be extremely heavy. Decide on a suitable section line, and cut the body in two with a damp palette knife. Then, with a strip tool, coiler, or any other suitable tool, hollow out as much clay as possible from each part. Coat the cut edges generously with slip, and press the two parts together again. Lute the joint thoroughly and make it good with extra clay.

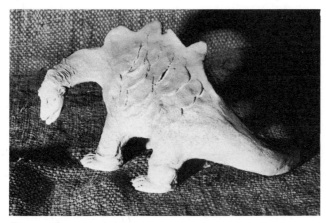

Fig. 72. *Completed animal.*

(4) A hole must be made underneath the belly to let air escape. If this is not done the piece will shatter, as air expands during firing.

(5) Now model on all the detail you think necessary to satisfy your original concept of the creature. A little slip should be used to link on any added parts.

(6) When modelling is complete, clean the model up with a damp sponge. Leave it to dry, ready for the biscuit-fire.

DECORATION

(1) Chosen areas can, if desired, be painted with coloured slips before biscuit-firing. Spattering these on will produce a gradated effect, as opposed to a flat colour.

(2) Glazing is entirely optional. A colourless, transparent glaze would suit a smooth, slimy creature. If coloured slips have not been used, an opaque, single-colour glaze could be used. Or you may decide that glaze is totally superfluous.

Fig. 73. *Prehistoric animals made by 13-year-old boys.*

Assignment 4 –
on the Wheel
Small Bowl

HAVING CONCENTRATED up to now on simple shapes based on a cylinder, the next step is making a bowl. The inside of a true bowl should have a perfect curve, however steep or shallow. A dish, however, has a flat bottom and is basically a large shallow cylinder.

Fig. 74. Types of bowl.

Before starting to throw a bowl, the concentration of clay for subsequent shaping must be considered, especially when a shallow form is required. Obviously, far more clay will be necessary to shape the top of the bowl, which has a large circumference, than the bottom where the circumference is small. Figs. 77 – 78 show how this is dealt with in the throwing process.

DESIGN

A number of points relating to a bowl's suitability for its intended purpose must be borne in mind when planning the design. If the bowl is for your own use, you are in a position to satisfy all your requirements.

For the first example, consider a cereal bowl. Bear in mind the quantity of cereal you normally eat, and whether you like a lot of milk. The bowl must be large enough for the cereal not to well over the top of the full bowl when a spoon is put in. Large cereals like Shredded Wheat may need a larger bowl, or one of a different shape.

For a grapefruit bowl, first find out the average size of a half grapefruit. Decide whether there should be any extra space around and above the grapefruit, and if so, how much. It might be an idea to try and incorporate in the design something to put the pips in.

If the bowl is for soup, decide whether the soup should cool quickly, or keep hot for some time. Shape is a decisive factor here. The bowl may need to be handled during use – the design might include lugs or handles. Think about a suitable shape from which to spoon out liquid.

WORK SEQUENCE

(1) Throw the ball of clay on to the moving wheel, centre it, and make the first opening.

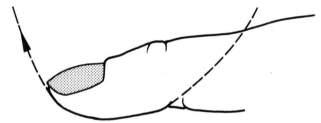

Fig. 75. The thumb has a natural shape for making bowls.

(2) The profile of the thumb has a natural curve which is invaluable in bowl making. Grip the left wrist with the right finger tips, put the left hand round the clay, and the right thumb inside the clay mass until it just reaches the bottom. Then move slowly but steadily upwards with both hands, allowing the natural curve of the thumb to make the shape. Reduce pressure as the top is reached so that the diameter does not become too large. This curve must remain throughout the making process; once lost, it is practically impossible to recreate.

(3) Since it is important at this stage to create height not width, lift and thin the clay wall. Relax pressure towards the top of the movement in order to maintain thickness in the upper portion of the wall – the area which will subsequently be stretched.

32

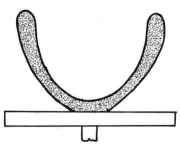

Fig. 76. *Section of a bowl, showing top thickness to allow for widening.*

Fig. 78. *Flattening the bowl. Note the position of the hands.*

Fig. 77. *Widening the bowl for the initial upright shape.*

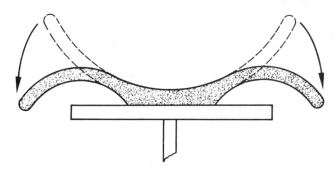

Fig. 79. *'Pancaking' as a result of over-widening the bowl.*

(4) Having achieved the required height, shape and widen the bowl by synchronous movement of the hands both outwards and upwards. Increased circumference will use up the extra clay thickness left at the top of the wall: when shaping is complete, the wall section should be of uniform thickness.

(5) For a very shallow bowl, lower the wall carefully by placing the left hand palm open on the outside, and the right hand palm open on the inside, and move both, very slowly, outwards and upwards. Do not overdo this, or the side will pancake.

(6) Trim the bowl with the side tool, and cut it from the wheel. When it has dried to leather-hard, turn the foot.

DECORATION

Stencils create an attractive decorative effect, and can easily be made from newspaper. The shape and size of the stencils will naturally depend on the piece itself, and the area of it to be decorated. Shallow soup bowls, for instance, are enhanced by an interesting inside decoration, but an upright sugar bowl is perhaps better decorated on the outside.

(1) Decide where the decoration is to be applied.

33

Fig. 80. Paper stencils.

(2) Using a wide soft brush, spin white slip on to the area to be decorated, and let it dry until no shine is evident.

(3) Experiment with ideas for the stencils, which must relate to the shape of the area to be decorated. It is useless, for example, to cut a stencil based on a large circle and expect it to lie flat and even in a steep-sided bowl.

Small units arranged in an all-over pattern are a suitable subject for a stencil. Alternatively, cut a small centre piece from a circle which has been twice folded before cutting. When opened out, it will form a symmetrical unit. Shapes based on sections of a circle (see Fig. 80) look very attractive on bowls and plates.

(4) Cut out the chosen stencil shape in newspaper. If the design calls for a number of identical shapes, these are best cut out as one from a pile of single sheets, to ensure uniformity.

(5) Soak the stencils in water.

(6) When they are supple, pick them out with tweezers and press them on to the slipped area.

(7) Using a spray diffuser, spray the whole slipped area

34

with a metallic oxide powder suspended in water, or else spatter the oxide from a stiff brush (old toothbrushes are ideal). Get someone to hold an open newspaper behind the pot to avoid undue mess.

(8) When the surplus moisture has dried off, lift the stencils from one corner and peel them away.

(9) Place the bowl on the drying rack, ready for firing.

(10) After biscuit-firing, cover with a transparent clear glaze, through which the pattern will shine out.

Fig. 81. Bowl with a newspaper stencil fixed ready for spraying (left), and the completed bowl (right).

Assignment 4 – off the Wheel

Devil's Mask

MANY PRIMITIVE tribes produce masks for the observance of their various rituals. There is an excellent collection of masks in the Horniman Museum at Forest Hill, London, which is well worth a visit. If it is not possible to visit a museum, the local public library may prove useful.

DESIGN

Ideas are best clarified by making a number of sketches and colouring them with paint or crayons. Decide on the general form and proportion of the mask, and whether or not hair is to be included. The clay can be pierced for eyes, nose, and mouth. Animal characteristics, such as horns, are often found on primitive masks, and something of this nature might be included.

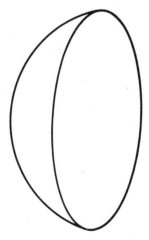

Fig. 82. Pinched 'blank' shape for devil's mask.

WORK SEQUENCE AND DECORATION

(1) Prepare a lump of clay roughly the same shape as the final mask, but slightly smaller.

(2) Using fingers and thumbs, squeeze a shallow depression in the clay mass as if making a thumb pot. Leave the walls quite thick at this stage, but model them to a shape like the vertical section of an egg.

(3) From the inside, push into relief any parts which should protrude, such as the nose and the chin. Do the same from the outside for those parts to be pushed inwards, such as nostrils and eyeballs.

(4) The clay will be too limp to take any further modelling at this stage without losing its shape. Crumple some tissue paper and fill the depressions that have been made for the features. Then put the mask aside to harden for a little while.

(5) When the work is resumed, add more detail by further modelling; adding extra clay where high relief is necessary; cutting into the clay with a knife or modelling tool, to give depth; and texturing some areas to create contrast and interest. Avoid drawing on the clay – it is always important to think in three-dimensional terms.

(7) When modelling is complete, remove the tissue paper packing and carve away as much surplus clay as possible with a wire modelling tool or a strip tool. This makes the piece lighter and less likely to crack or shatter during firing. Watch the contour of the mask when doing this; the inside shape should correspond roughly to that of the outside.

(8) If the mask is to be hung on a wall, make some provision for this.

(9) Paint the mask with coloured slips like those used for the jug in Assignment 3. Remember that slip can be scratched through to produce special effects.

(10) Put the mask aside to dry, ready for biscuit-firing.

(11.) Apply a transparent glaze, if desired.

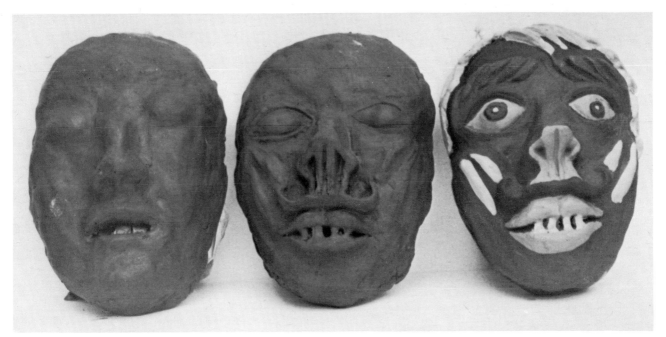

Fig. 83. Three stages in modelling a devil's mask.

Assignment 5 –
on the Wheel

Pot with a Simple Lid

SOME ARTICLES, SUCH as pots to contain food, need a lid, and a number of different types will be described in this book. Look round at home and in china shops, and jot down sketches of as many types as possible. Some are quite complicated, but this assignment shows how to make a very simple covered jam pot.

DESIGN

The pot will consist of a container with a flanged top, in which will sit a flat lid. A 'sit-in' type of lid is quite satisfactory here, since the pot will not be tipped (as a teapot would), and the lid does not therefore need to be held firmly in place. Think carefully about shape and size. Remember that some jam spoons are wider than teaspoons. Experiment with folded white card, as in Assignment 2, to produce a final card mock-up. If you want to make a handle or knob for the flat lid, consider the various forms possible. The lid will frequently be put back on the pot with the spoon still inside: decide how this can best be done.

WORK SEQUENCE

For all the work to date, a red earthenware clay body has been used. This pot is made in white earthenware body, which is very silky to touch, but not quite so 'good-tempered', and a little less plastic.
(1) Throw the pot to the shape and size of the card cut-out, and keep the top rim fairly thick.
(2) Make sure the rim is running perfectly true on the wheel. If not, cut it level with a needle, as illustrated in Assignment 1.

Fig. 84. Using a ruler to form a flange at the top of the pot.

(3) Take a short ruler, or anything similar with a square-cut end, wet it, and then hold it vertically between the finger tips in front and the thumbs behind. Brace your arms to your body, and let the end of the wet ruler meet the thickness of the rim about half-way across. Gradually feed the ruler down into the clay until the required depth of flange has been reached. The pressed-down clay makes a neat overhanging flange on the inside. In some cases the ruler will need to be tilted a little, either to the inside or to the outside.

This operation looks as though it takes a lot of practice, but it is really quite simple.
(4) Trim the foot, sponge, and cut from the wheel.
(5) Set the callipers to $\frac{1}{8}$ in. (3 mm.) less than the size of the flange (this is to allow for glazing). Measure this diameter, and then use compasses to mark and cut out a circle of this size in card.
(6) Roll out a flat slab of clay about $\frac{1}{4}$ in. (6 mm.) thick and, using the card as a template, cut out a clay circle the same size.
(7) Prepare the handle, if you are going to have one.
(8) Let all three parts become leather-hard. Now turn a foot on the pot, and slip and lute the handle on to the

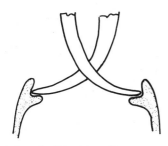

Fig. 85. Measuring the lid with callipers.

Fig. 86. Lid in place. Notice the gaps at the side to allow for glaze thickness.

middle of the flat circle. If you want, cut a recess in the lid for a spoon. Sponge the pieces to leave soft edges.
(9) Allow the pot and lid to dry, and then biscuit-fire them.

DECORATION

Decoration has up to now always been applied before the biscuit-fire. This time it is to be applied to the biscuit-fired pot before it is glazed. This is known as under-glaze decoration. It will not wear away when the article is used, as does the on-glaze decoration on many plates found in the home.
(1) Take a paintbrush and some colours, and experiment with the form the brushwork is to take. Once again, consider the shape. The decoration might consist of a pair of simple side motifs, a border, some vertically spaced lines, or simple rings spun round on the banding-wheel.
(2) Pencil on the biscuited pot any guide-lines necessary – these will burn away later.

(3) Grind some under-glaze colour with a few drops of under-glaze medium, using a palette knife on a glass slab. The medium is a siccative to prevent the dried colour from smudging when glazed. If under-glaze medium is not available, grind the colour with a little water and add a few drops of gum arabic.
(4) Paint the pattern on the biscuit. Use a full brush, as the best results are obtained from clean, well-defined strokes, and the biscuit is, of course, porous.

Fig. 87. Pot and lid ready for the biscuit-fire (left), and the biscuited pot, decorated with under-glaze colours (right).

(5) Let the paints dry thoroughly, and then glaze with a colourless transparent glaze.

Assignment 5 – off the Wheel

Shallow Dish

SHALLOW DISHES AND plates can be made using a very simple type of plaster former. This is sometimes called a flop-over or hump mould, though a mould is technically something in which a liquid is cast. A variety of shapes is possible, and this type of dish can be used, for instance, for small pats of butter, as a cucumber dish, as small plates, or as an ash tray. If you have a knowledge of woodwork, you might consider making a set of hors d'oeuvre dishes and a wooden tray to stand them on.

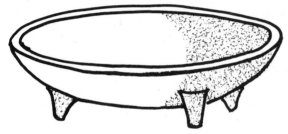

Fig. 88. Feet may be fitted to the dish if required.

DESIGN

Size and shape will vary widely, depending on the purpose for which the dish is to be used. Short feet can be added to the dish, if desired.

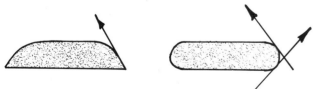

Fig. 89. Suitable (left), and unsuitable undercut shapes for casting.

Make a cardboard cut-out of the mouth shape of the proposed dish, and a template of its elevation. The shape of the elevation must become increasingly wider towards the bottom, since a plaster impression cannot be taken from a mass which is undercut. If you have access to a metal workshop, reproduce the side template in tin plate, as it is easier to work with, and can also be used as a scraper.

WORK SEQUENCE

(1) Place the plan shape on a board, and hump some clay on it. Model this clay to the form of the proposed dish, inverted. Use the template to check this. Make sure the top of the hump remains level and flat – a wet piece of wood used on edge, as in concrete levelling, is useful.

(2) Surround the hump with a casting-box, or erect a suitable wall of linoleum or roofing felt (this wall is known as a cottle). Seal all the joints with clay.

(3) Push the cardboard tube from a toilet roll about $\frac{3}{16}$ in. (5 mm.) deep into a soft lump of clay.

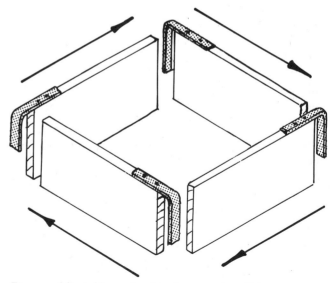

Fig. 90. Adjustable casting-box for a number of sizes.

Fig. 91. Shaping the clay hump with a tin plate template.

(4) Mix and pour sufficient plaster to embed the hump to a minimum depth of about $1\frac{1}{4}$ in. (30 mm.), and fill the tube as well.

(5) When set, remove the clay lump and the cardboard tube, and let the plaster harden.

Fig. 92. Modelled clay shape ready for the plaster pour.

Fig. 93. Filling a cardboard roll with plaster.

41

(6) Thoroughly soap-size the cast. Mix enough plaster to fill the recess left by the clay lump. Tap the container of plaster a few times to remove any air bubbles.
(7) When the plaster is just on the turn, push the plaster cylinder vertically into it; make sure that it does not penetrate too far and so touch the plaster waste mould beneath. Hold it still for a few minutes until the plaster is sufficiently set to support it on its own. Reinforce the joint with any remaining plaster, using it as a mason would, in the thick, mortar state.
(8) Give this plaster time to become really hard. Then plunge the whole lot into a sink or bucket of cold water. After a little while the two portions can be pulled apart.
(9) Clean up any irregularities on the bottom edge with a piece of glasspaper.
(10) Roll out a pancake of clay $\frac{1}{4}$ in. (6 mm.) thick on a piece of cloth (sacking is excellent). Get someone to hold the flop-over former upright on the table (this is the reason for making the plaster handle). Now pick up the clay on the material, invert it so that the sacking is on top, lift it above the former, and flop it on to the plaster. This action makes the clay begin to take on the required shape. Complete the shaping, especially towards the rim, by patting lightly with the palm of the hand through the cloth.
(11) When the clay is the same shape as the former, peel off the material. This will leave an attractive texture.
(12) Cut away the surplus clay with a damp knife.
(13) Allow the clay to 'freeze' into shape – this will take a while, though the porous plaster will help. When the clay is ready, lift it from the former.
(14) Clean and sponge the cut edge.
(15) Biscuit-fire the dish when dry.

DECORATION

One attractive way to decorate a dish is to use what is best described as a 'reflected image' pattern. The idea is to make one half light on dark, and the other a mirror image of it, dark on light. Fig. 96 illustrates this.

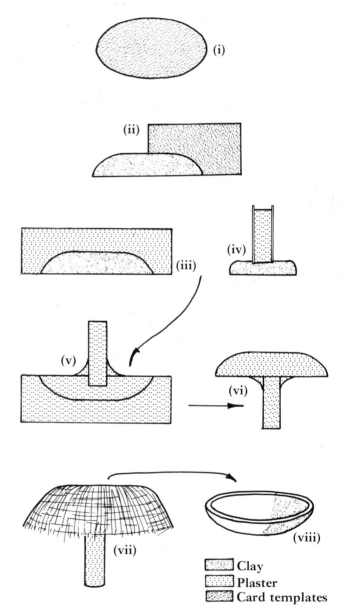

Clay
Plaster
Card templates

Fig. 94. Stages in making a flop-over dish: (i) the plan template, (ii) shaping the solid clay with the side template, (iii) casting the waste mould, (iv) casting the handle, (v) and (vi) casting the full mould, (vii) flopping over the clay on the hessian, and (viii) the finished dish.

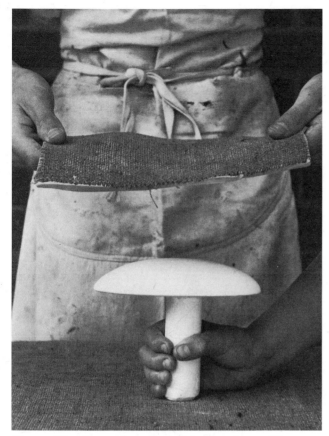

Fig. 95. The clay ready to 'pancake' on to the mould.

Fig. 96. A reflected image pattern.

Fig. 97. Casting from the waste mould. The handle is held in position until the plaster sets.

Fig. 98. The inside (right), and outside (left) of the completed dish. The clay is shown flopped over the mould (centre).

43

(1) Design a pattern which suits the shape of the dish, and possibly also bears some relation to its intended use.

(2) Draw it in pencil on the biscuited dish.

(3) Mix up some under-glaze colour, as described in the first section of this assignment, and paint the pattern in the appropriate areas.

(4) Allow the decoration to dry thoroughly, and then glaze the dish with a colourless transparent glaze.

Assignment 6 – on the Wheel

Pot with a Thrown Lid

THIS SHOULD BE AN easy progression from the marmalade jar in Assignment 5, which was fitted with a flat slab lid resting on a flange inside. This pot also has a simple sit-in lid, but this time the lid itself is to be shaped on the wheel.

Fig. 99. Section through covered pot and lid.

DESIGN

This type of lid produces a better line between lid and pot, and allows the lid and its grip to be made as one piece. There are many uses for a lidded pot, such as a sweet jar, a butter dish, a honey pot, or a pickle jar.

Decide on a sensible size related to the pot's intended use, and make some progressive sketches of the pot and its lid.

WORK SEQUENCE

(1) Prepare two balls of clay, one for the pot and one for the lid.

(2) Throw the pot, and make the rim for the lid exactly as before.

(3) Take a calliper measurement of the inner rim size.

(4) Cut the pot, and lift it from the wheel.

(5) Centre the small piece of clay for the lid. The lid is made upside down (it will finish as an inverted cone shape), so the knob portion need not be large.

(6) In the top of this clay throw a small bowl (see Assignment 4) to the shape designed, and check the mouth size against the calliper measurement. If it is too small, extra widening is easy. If too large, the best remedy is to cut off a portion and re-shape. Clean the base with a side tool, and cut the lid from the wheel.

(7) Turn the pot in the usual way.

(8) Now turn the lid, as follows. Centre the lid rim on the wheel, and fasten it down with three small pieces of clay. Using a flat turning tool, make the top perfectly true and slightly concave. Remove the lid from the wheel, re-centre it, and fasten it mouth-upwards. In this position you can check the fit by inverting the pot over it. If the lid is too big, turn away a little of the bowl and check the fit again. Remember to allow a little clearance as both lid and pot are to be glazed. When the lid is the right size, re-centre it the right way up and fasten it down. Using a coiler and a flat turning tool, make the surplus clay on top into a cylindrical mass of the same diameter as the knob at its widest point. With suitably shaped turning tools, cut into this cylinder the shape required for the knob. Sponge the lid and remove it from the wheel, then clean up any untidy remains of the fastening clay.

(9) Let the pieces dry, and biscuit-fire them.

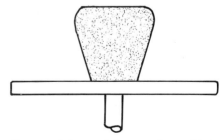

Fig. 100. Suggested shape of the mass from which to start throwing a lid.

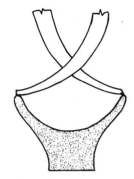

Fig. 101. Checking the calliper measurement of the lid to ensure a perfect fit.

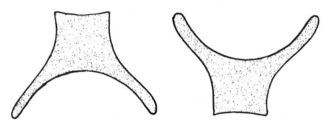

Fig. 102. First and second stages in turning a lid.

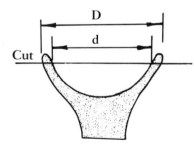

Fig. 103. Method of reducing the diameter of the lid.

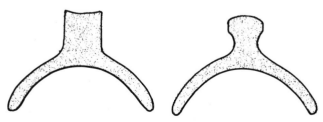

Fig. 104. Third and fourth stages in turning a lid.

45

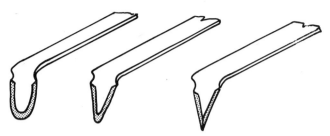

Fig. 105. Types of turning tool.

Fig. 106. Shaping the lid with a turning tool.

DECORATION

Design a coloured unit decoration or border, including lines spun on the banding-wheel if desired.

(1) Weigh out a quantity of transparent glaze, and add ten per cent of its weight in stannic oxide powder. Grind these together dry in a pestle, add water, regrind and sieve as described on page 121.

(2) This mixture is known as a majolica or tin enamel glaze. In Assignment 5 you painted on the biscuit and then covered it with glaze. This time you can paint on the glaze before it is fired. To colour the majolica, use specially formulated tin enamel colours; these must be ground with a little water on a glass slab, using a

Fig. 107. Pot and un-turned lid (right), and the completed piece (left), tin-glazed and decorated with majolica colours, ready for the glaze-fire.

palette knife, and then diluted to the required tone. Alternatively, you can use small quantities of raw oxides, well diluted with water.

(3) Painting the pattern on the glazed pot is not easy. The surface will be powdery and porous and it will feel like painting on blotting paper (in fact, painting on blotting paper is excellent preparation for this!). To produce a clean line, use a very full brush. Try to complete each stroke in one movement. Be very careful how you handle the pot while glazing it, as this glaze is easily smudged.

(4) Glaze-fire. The under-side of the lid must be free of glaze if it is fired directly on the shelf. The result will be quite different from under-glaze painting, for the colours will have merged slightly with the glaze, and the edges of the pattern will look soft and delicately blurred. This is the technique which was practised by the famous Dutch tile painters.

46

Assignment 6 – off the Wheel

Figurine

No DOUBT AT SOME time or other you have drawn matchstick men as a simple way of indicating movement and action. Perhaps you have made 'movie' pictures by drawing matchstick men on consecutive page edges of a notebook, each with the action slightly changed, so that a quick flick through with the fingers gives the impression of actual movement.

DESIGN

Using the same matchstick man system, make some sketches of a person engaged on an easily recognisable

Fig. 108. Initial 'matchstick' drawings.

activity, such as playing a musical instrument; sitting down reading the paper; at a work bench; or playing tennis. Now look at all these action sketches and imagine them, not as pencil lines, but as rolls of clay; that is as three-dimensional pieces. Plastic clay, as you will now realise, cannot easily support itself. Looking at your sketches, decide which of the figures could stand up if made in clay, and which would need some kind of support. Make any necessary additions to the sketches, or change the pose if it will aid stability. A seated person is a safer proposition than a standing figure, which will require a prop to make it stable.

From these preliminary sketches choose one which looks as if it will model well, and then decide on size. The bigger the figure, the more difficult it will be to manipulate. Very tiny figures, on the other hand, can prove tedious.

Fig. 109. Stages in making a roll and ball figure.

WORK SEQUENCE AND DECORATION

(1) Prepare a fairly thick roll of clay for the trunk; a thinner roll long enough for both legs; another, still thinner, long enough for both arms; and a small roll for the neck. The head is a small ball of clay made in the palms of the hands.

(2) Cut the rolls to the right length and arrange them on a piece of paper as shown in Fig. 109. Join the parts with slip and lute them well together.

(3) Prepare any props required, and join and lute any pieces which form part of these props.

(4) Pick up your clay figure and copy the pose from the sketch. The body, arms, and legs will bend quite easily while the clay is still soft and plastic. Incorporate the props, if any, and mount the whole model on a clay base.

(5) Leave the assembly to dry a little, until it holds its shape.

Simple action figures like this can be quite attractive if fired and glazed, but will be much more interesting if clothed.

(6) Using thin plywood strips as slats, prepare a flat pancake of clay.

(7) Cut some pieces of clothing from newspaper, and fit them on the clay figure. Sleeves and trouser legs can be cut separately, and hats can be built up from two or more pieces.

(8) Using these newspaper patterns as templates, cut the clothes from the pancake of clay and model them round the figure. Where edges meet, join them with a little slip before modelling them together.

(9) Having joined on the main clothes, add any other suitable details, for example beads, pockets, a tie, or an umbrella, to make your composition interesting and complete.

(10) Simple details may be added to the head. Tiny pats of clay can represent features. Pats of clay or small rolls are useful to suggest hair.

(11) Allow to dry. Biscuit-fire.

(12) In Assignment 5, under-glaze colours were used. The figure can be decorated with these, if used sparingly. If overdone, the effect is lost completely.

Assignment 7 – on the Wheel

Flat-Bottomed Dish

IN ASSIGNMENT 6 ONE modification of the simple cylinder was described – shaping the rim to form a flange. Another possibility is to make the cylinder very short and wide. This constitutes a dish, and the sides can be left straight, or splayed inwards or outwards. Small dishes can be made that are both attractive and functional.

DESIGN

Decide on a size to meet your particular requirement, which might be for a tray to hold drawing pins, a dish for nuts or biscuits, or an individual butter or jam dish for breakfast in bed.

WORK SEQUENCE

(1) Start throwing from a low but wide-centred lump of clay, and make the initial opening with the right thumb.

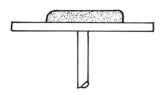

Fig. 110. Shape of the clay mass from which to start a flat, shallow dish.

(2) The movement to widen the mass (see Assignment 1) must be exaggerated, so that most of the clay is taken up in the formation of the base.

(3) The short side is then thinned, shaped, and if necessary cut down to size.

Cutting a dish of this sort from the wheel presents problems, as it tends to buckle. One solution is to leave it to harden a little on the wheel before cutting free. Small plastic bats are useful if you have them – use a small quantity of clay to fix one to the wheel by suction, so that when throwing is completed the dish can be removed on the bat and left to dry. Some pottery suppliers make rubber tile bats which are ideal for this purpose.

(4) Trim and turn the foot when ready.

(5) If you wish to change the basic shape of the dish, it can be converted from a round thrown dish into an oval one like this. First cut the thrown dish from the wheel, and lift it carefully on to a piece of thickish paper on a smooth flat board. Now cut a small elongated diamond-shaped piece out of the centre. Cover the edges of the gap with slip, and then press the sides of the dish together with both hands until the diamond is fully closed. Finish by modelling the sides of the incision together, levelling them, and sponging the dish.

DECORATION

A flat surface like the inside of this dish is an ideal one on which to experiment with combing. This decorative method was much used by the early Staffordshire slipware potters.

(1) A slip trailer is used for this technique. In appearance and function it is not unlike a cake icing syringe. It consists of a flat rubber bag, the opening of which forms a long tube designed to hold a piece of drawn-out glass tubing. By varying the nozzle size of the glass tube, the slip can be made to form different shapes on the article it is decorating.

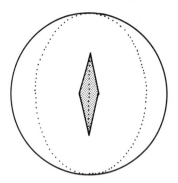

Fig. 111. *Cutting out a diamond to make a round dish into an oval one*

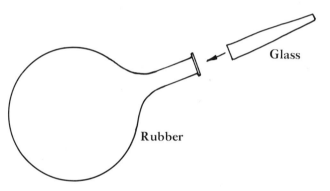

Fig. 112. *Slip trailer.*

Fig. 113. *Plastic hypodermic syringe suitable for filling a slip trailer.*

49

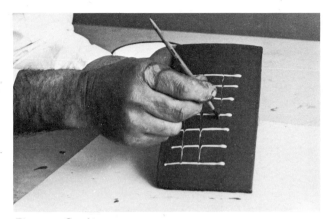

Fig. 114. Combing.

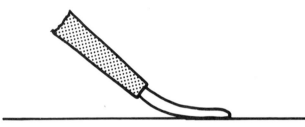

Fig. 115. Slip falling on to the clay from the slip trailer.

(2) Prepare and sieve both white and brown slip, and fill the trailer with some of the white, using a plastic syringe.

(3) Dilute the brown slip with water and beat it well until it is free-flowing. Swill the inside of the dish with it, draining off the surplus from the edge.

(4) Using the trailer as shown in Fig. 115, let trails or pipings of the white slip fall on to the brown-slipped dish. Do not touch the brown slip with the glass trailer nozzle.

(5) Take a bristle, a feather, or a camel-hair brush, damp it, and flatten it between the fingers. Draw tickling surface lines across the top of the slip at right angles to the trailed piping. Rest your right hand on your flat left arm, as if it were a painter's maul stick.

Leave a space of about $\frac{5}{8}$ in. (15 mm.) between each stroke. Turn the dish completely round, and make a second set of light strokes between the first set. The overall appearance should be a sequence of double ogee curves at the points where the implement crosses the white trailed lines.

The wet slip will make the dish very damp, so leave it on paper to harden slowly (sudden drying out can lead to cracking, so avoid direct sunlight or radiators).

If, in future work, you would like to try something more intricate, try spinning a slipped dish on the banding-wheel to trail a continuous spiral from the centre to the outside. Follow this by combing in radial fashion from the centre to the outside.

(6) Biscuit-fire the dish when it is completely dry.

(7) Finish with a coloured transparent glaze.

Fig. 116. Dishes decorated with combing.

Assignment 7 –
off the Wheel

Sugar Basin

CRAFTSMEN WORKING FOR instance in sheet metal, making cardboard models, or using stitchery as their means of artistic expression, often make up three-dimensional objects with a development as the starting point for a project. A development is the shape obtained after opening out all the sides of a three-dimensional figure and laying them flat to produce a two-dimensional form. Since most clay is a plastic medium, ceramic articles can be made in the same way.

When learning any new technique, it is sensible to start with something relatively simple, but although this sugar basin is easy to make, it is interesting and unusual because it has flat sides as a change from the usual round pot.

DESIGN

Think first about size – the height of the basin and the amount of sugar you want it to contain. Within the brief of straight lines, the basin can be straight-sided, splayed, or converged. Remember that the sugar basin should be stable, and although sugar should not spill out easily, it must be easily spooned out.

Design scope is also widened by varying the number of sides, but as too many sides would prove complicated for the beginner, it may be best to keep to four.

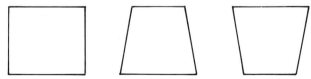

Fig. 117. Alternative elevations for developed sides.

WORK SEQUENCE

(1) Using a drawing board, T square and set square, draw the development of the chosen shape on a piece of thin card. A specimen development is illustrated in Fig. 120.

(2) Cut this out with scissors.

(3) Roll out a flat piece of clay to $\frac{1}{4}$ in. (6 mm.) thickness, place the card development on top, and roll the clay once or twice more to anchor it on to the clay.

It is often easier to start rolling with two clay masses crossed one over the other (see Fig. 118).

(4) Cut round the template with a damp knife.

(5) Lift the cut shape carefully, and turn it over so that the clay rests upon the card.

(6) Trim the joining edges to make a mitre fit possible.

(7) Gradually lift the first side, with the card still adhering to it (a small piece of hardboard or thick card will assist in obtaining a straight tip-up from the bottom). The card template will hold the side in its new position, and keep it flat. Raise the other sides in sequence, leaving a small gap at the joining edges.

(8) Coat these joint edges well with slip and squeeze them together, pinching each side lightly on the card.

(9) Lute these joints with a modelling tool on the inside. A little reinforcing roll of clay can be added to give rounded corners to the inside.

(10) Peel the cards off the sides, and complete the luting of the joints from the outside.

(11) Check that the pot is regular, and then leave it on the template to harden.

(12) When the pot is hard enough to handle, true the sides by laying each in turn on a flat paper-covered surface, and smoothing the inside with a flat piece of stick. Any outside modelling marks or depressions can be removed while the pot is upright. Sponge the pot, and keep it in the damp cupboard or wrapped in polythene.

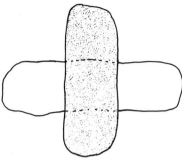

Fig. 118. Arrangement of clay roughly to match the given basin development.

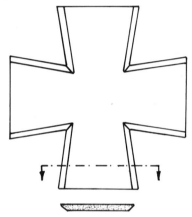

Fig. 119. Mitring the rolled out clay corners.

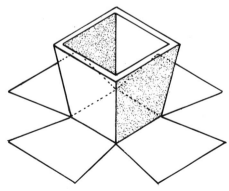

Fig. 120. Card template peeled off after the corners of the pot have been luted together.

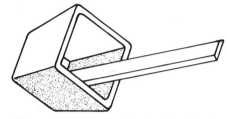

Fig. 121. Flattening the inside of a developed basin with a flat wooden ruler.

DECORATION

The outside can be decorated with a few well-chosen lines of trailing. Let the slip fall on to the clay surface from the slip trailer so that no mark is left by the glass tube. As the slip is wetter than the clay on which it is being used, a short period in the damp cupboard for readjustment is amply rewarded, and obviates the risk of the piping cracking away.

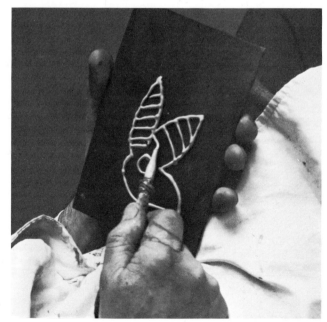

Fig. 122. Slip trailing.

Fig. 123. Making the pattern fit the shape.

Fig. 124. Stages in forming a developed sugar basin.

Dry the sugar basin slowly after this period of readjustment, and then biscuit-fire it. Glaze the piece with any transparent glaze, either clear or coloured.

Assignment 8 – on and off the Wheel

Combined Jug and Lemon Squeezer

THIS PIECE COMBINES a lemon squeezer and a jug to collect the juice. It brings together a number of skills and techniques already described, and introduces some new ones.

If a wheel is not available, the components thrown on the wheel can be made using flop-over moulds (see Assignments 5 and 9); alternatively they can be made rectangular in shape, using the development method (see Assignment 7).

DESIGN

Many people using the conventional glass or plastic lemon squeezer are frustrated by the tiny space round the actual squeezer part for collecting the juice. Too often this is inadequate even for a single lemon, and if a number of lemons or oranges are to be squeezed for cooking or making drinks, the squeezer has to be continually emptied. More often than not the pips are poured out with the juice. This composite jug and squeezer is intended to overcome all these basic design faults.

You will need to know the size and basic shape of the average half lemon; also the average size of a lemon pip, as you will have to make holes slightly smaller than this so that only the juice falls through.

Consider the ways in which the two parts might be locked together during use so that one does not turn in the other. Remember that the size of the mouth of the jug will be dependent on the size of the squeezer. The lip of the jug will present a problem. Because of

53

the flange it cannot be finger-pulled as in Assignment 3.

When these essential sizes and shapes have been established, remember to add one-tenth more to offset the shrinkage of the clay. Make a full size sectional drawing on white card of the whole assembly, and incorporate in it your solutions to the problems posed. One set of solutions is shown in Fig. 125. However the design problems have been overcome, the basic techniques will be similar.

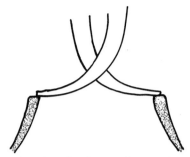
Fig. 126. *Ensuring that the thrown diameter is adequate before making the flange.*

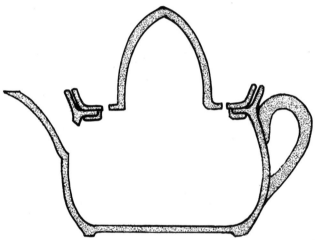
Fig. 125. *Section through the complete jug and squeezer.*

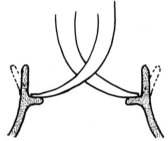
Fig. 127. *Checking the flange diameter ; the dotted lines show the position of the splay.*

WORK SEQUENCE ON THE WHEEL

(1) Throw the jug on the wheel (see Assignment 3) to the shape and size detailed in the sectional drawing. Remember to keep the top reasonably thick so that the flange can be made safely. Use the callipers, set direct from the card drawing, to ensure that the diameter of the flange will be adequate for seating the squeezer portion.

(2) Using a short wooden ruler, press down the flange and shape the rim with the fingers to the necessary splay (see Assignment 5). Check on the diameter again, since corrections can be made quite easily at this stage.

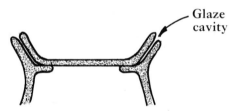
Glaze cavity

Fig. 128. *Correct size and fit for a sit-in lid.*

Fig. 129. *Development of the lip.*

54

(3) Trim the base with the side tool. Cut the jug from the wheel, and put it aside.

(4) Throw the base of the squeezer as a small flat-bottomed dish (see Assignment 7), and shape the relatively short sides to correspond to the splay on the top of the jug. Use the callipers to check that the internal size is correct. It is advisable at this stage to leave the wall of the dish a little thick so that it can be turned, since its base is doubling as a jug lid.

(5) When both jug and dish are leather-hard, turn the base of the dish flat, and turn the wall so that it fits loosely on to the flange of the jug. Remember to leave a small glaze clearance. Turn the foot of the jug.

(6) Next fit a handle to the jug. It can be made in either of the ways described in Assignments 1 and 3.

(7) A lip must now be made, and here is one solution to the problem.

Cut out a card template of a developed lip, bend it, and check the shape against the jug. If this first template is not ideal, experiment with further templates until a satisfactory form is obtained. Roll out a thin slab of clay on a piece of cartridge paper, and cut from it the shape of the template. Bend this shape to the required curvature, and let it dry to the same state as the jug. When ready, trim this lip piece to a snug fit against the jug. Cover the joint with slip, and model the lip on. The line it takes where it joins on to the jug must be smooth and graceful.

(8) Pierce a hole below the jug flange within the bounds of this modelled-on lip, and make a stream-lined inside link with the jug wall to make the juice flow easily.

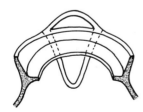

Fig. 130. Piercing the jug to facilitate the flow of juice into the lip.

WORK SEQUENCE OFF THE WHEEL, AND DECORATION

(1) Make a paper template of the basic shape of the actual squeezer pillar, plus a waste piece, as shown in Fig. 132. The waste piece should be about $\frac{1}{8}$ in. (3 mm.) thick.

(2) Obtain a piece of tin plate, and stick the paper template on to it with Cow gum. Cut round the paper with either flat or curved tin snips, according to shape, to produce a new template in tin plate. Flatten this on a table with a wooden mallet.

(3) Cut from a piece of $\frac{1}{8}$ in. (3 mm.) thick hardboard a circle of diameter equivalent to the waste piece (see Fig. 132); make a small hole through its centre with a bradawl. Cut off the head portion of a 1 in. (24 mm.) wire nail to a length of $\frac{7}{8}$ in. (20 mm.). Pass it through the hole in the centre of the circle and into a corresponding hole in a larger, thicker circle of wood, so that one rotates freely on the other.

(4) Stick a cylindrical lump of clay on to the round piece of hardboard, and model it roughly to the shape of the template. A perfect shape can now be obtained by holding the tin plate template upright with the right hand, while turning the clay against it with the left hand. This will scrape away surplus clay. If a hollow is exposed, extra clay can be added and subsequently scraped too.

(5) Put the finished pillar on one side to harden.

(6) When the pillar can be handled safely, cut a thin strip of paper, bend it round the base of the pillar and cut it to the exact circumference. Remove this paper and mark on it eight equal spaces. This is easily done by folding the paper three times, and making the marks on the creases formed. Put the paper strip back on the base of the pillar, and transfer the division marks to the clay. With the aid of a tri-square or set square join these marks to the apex of the pillar.

This method of division is very useful when decorating pottery, and is worth remembering.

55

Fig. 131. Components of the jug: the pot, the lip, the handle, and the lid.

Fig. 133. Simple forming jig for making the squeezer (centre), a card template (left), and a tin plate template shown against a formed clay shape (right).

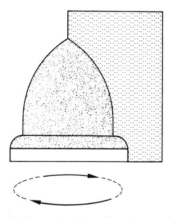

Fig. 132. The thickness of the hardboard must be included in the template shape.

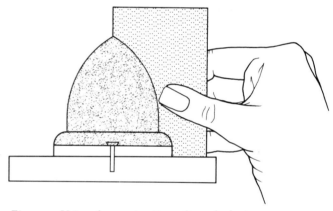

Fig. 134. Using the turning jig to form the basic squeezer.

(7) Between these lines cut tapering facets with a small knife, to produce a curved octagonal pyramid. Hollow each facet slightly with a modelling tool to produce a series of sharp edges. Finish by cleaning up with the sponge.

(8) Remove the round piece of hardboard, and put it waste side downwards on a flat piece of wood (offcuts of blockboard or thick plywood are ideal). Now erect round the clay a cottle, which must be at least $1\frac{5}{8}$ in. (40 mm.) higher, and $3\frac{1}{4}$ in. (80 mm.) greater in diameter than the clay. Many materials are suitable, for

example a strip of thin linoleum or a strip of roofing felt; for small pieces such as this, a cottle can be made from a thick rolled out piece of clay. Tie the cottle round with string, or, if made of clay, model it well together. Make a clay seal both at the junction and at the place where the cottle joins the base, to ensure that it is completely waterproof.

(9) Mix the plaster (see Assignment 5), and pour it into the cottle. Agitate the plaster to disperse any air bubbles round the clay, and leave it to set.

(10) When the plaster is hard, remove the cottle and

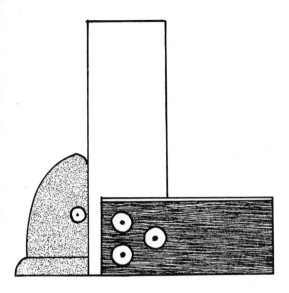

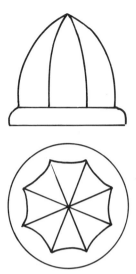

Fig. 136. Marking the flutes.

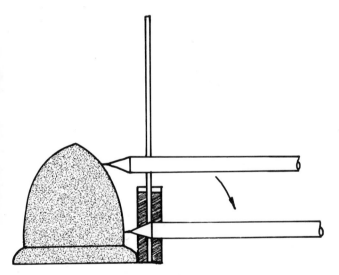

Fig. 135. Using a tri-square to assist in drawing vertical lines on a curved surface.

Fig. 137. Cottle in position and clay-sealed at the base.

the base board and carefully extract the clay, taking care not to damage the inside surface of the plaster. The end product is known as a one-piece drain mould, which is regularly used in pottery for casting shapes with only one direction of curve. Any number of lemon squeezer pillars can be made from this mould.

(11) Fill the mould with deflocculated casting-slip. Allow it to stand for about twenty minutes (slightly less if the mould is very dry, and slightly longer if the mould is damp). Then pour out any slip which has still not adhered to the porous wall of the mould, and leave it

57

Fig. 138. Casting the squeezer. Note that the waste rim is trimmed away after casting.

to drain on a pair of slats over a bucket. The mould will continue to dry out the clay, and after a little while the cast can be lifted from the mould.

(12) Where the casting dripped its surplus clay, an uneven edge will have been created. This was why a waste piece was added, which can now be removed with a damp knife.

(13) Join the squeezer pillar to the inside of the flat dish with casting-slip, turn the assembly over, and cut away the centre of the dish base below and inside the pillar. This makes it possible to lute the two pieces together with a modelling tool (luting on the outside would damage the shape). Cutting away the centre also allows air to escape from inside the pillar during firing.

(14) The jug and the pillar must somehow be locked together when in use. One solution is to model two small blocks of clay on to the outer edge of the dish base, and to cut corresponding recesses in the jug rim, so that the two register. The best position for the pieces of clay and the recesses is at right angles to the axis of the lip and handle.

(15) Puncture the rim to allow the juice (but not the pips) to pass through into the jug. These outlets can be either small holes or fine curved slits.

(16) Set the piece aside to dry; biscuit-fire it.

(17) Use an opaque glaze.

Fig. 139. Completed jug and squeezer.

Assignment 9 – on the Wheel

Small Bottle

WHEN SHAPING A THROWN cylinder, it is far easier to belly it out than to gather it in. This bottle-shaped piece provides practice in gathering-in, which is essential if you are to give full expression to your design ideas.

DESIGN

The basic bottle shape has a very restricted and gathered-in neck. Your design can be as individual as you like, provided this feature is retained.

A pair of bottles for vinegar and olive oil is one suggestion that might be considered, but a bottle shape does not have to serve as a bottle, and a slim vase for a single rose would be very attractive. Work out the most suitable size and shape, and decide whether a lip is required. If a handle is necessary, what type should it be? Consider the possibility of making a tip-over top to combine a lip and a grip. A cork will be needed if the bottle is to contain anything edible, and the neck will therefore have to be made to a certain size.

Make some sketches, and cut them out in card and stand them up if this is helpful.

Fig. 140. Running lip.

WORK SEQUENCE

(1) Estimate the amount of clay needed. Throw and centre the clay, and adjust the size of the lump as necessary.
(2) Make the first entry with the thumb as before, and widen it to the required base size.

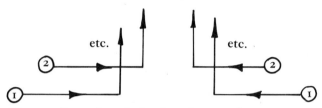

Fig. 141. Stages in gathering-in a thrown neck.

Fig. 142. A bottle is basically cone-shaped.

(3) Clearly, if the top of the pot is to be very narrow, it should be kept as narrow as possible from the start. With this in mind, press rather more heavily with the right hand than with the left when raising the wall. In this way a hollow cone is produced, instead of the customary cylinder. However the top must still be sufficiently large at this stage for the fingers of the left hand to work inside.
(4) When the wall is thick enough, shape the lower portion, which will prove impossible once the neck is made.

59

Fig. 143. Gathering-in the neck.

(5) Gathering-in the top requires very carefully controlled shaping. Fig. 143 shows the right movement to use. Bend the last three fingers of each hand towards the body. Place the backs of the middle fingers, just behind the first joint, on either side of the neck. Curve the first fingers round the neck at the back, and place the thumbs, tips touching, on the rim of the neck at the front. This restricts the clay at six contact points, and helps to prevent buckling. Give the clay a little pinch, and then raise the fingers slowly and vertically to the top. This will reduce the diameter and thicken the wall correspondingly. Repeat this as many times as necessary, but the action must always be a little squeeze and a slow vertical lift; continual pushing inwards right to the top will end in disaster.

When the wall becomes too thick as a result of this action, use the same movement as for raising the wall, but confine it to the thickened neck area. The two actions should follow in sequence:

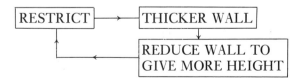

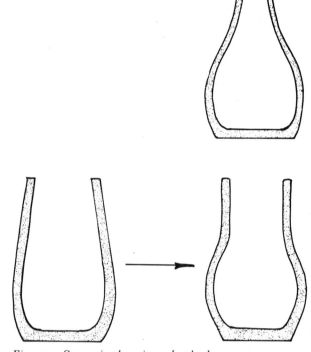

Fig. 144. Stages in throwing a bottle shape.

Keep your arms well to your side while gathering-in the neck, to avoid developing a wobble.

(6) Trim the outside. If a lip is required, pull one. Remove the bottle from the wheel, and allow it to dry to leather-hard.

(7) Turning the foot presents a problem, for the bottle will not stay upside down on the wheel, balancing on a tiny neck rim. Thick cone-shaped rings of leather-hard clay are required: choose one of suitable size, centre it, and fasten it on to the wheel with clay. It is wise to test it for truth with the turning tool.

(8) Invert the bottle neck-down on to the ring, and make sure your eyes are level with the base of the bottle. Now move the bottle until it appears true. Spin the wheel to see if the bottle is running concentrically

within the ring. If not, stop the wheel, adjust, and test again, repeating until the bottle is centred.

(9) Once centred, hold the bottle so that it cannot move, and fasten it to the ring with clay.

(10) The base can now be turned in the usual manner. Avoid too much pressure, as this might cause movement within the ring. When turning is complete, the bottle and the ring can be separated and both tidied up.

(11) Make and fit a handle, if desired.

(12) Dry the bottle, and biscuit-fire it.

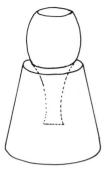

Fig. 146. Using a turning ring when making the foot of the narrow-necked bottle.

DECORATION

(1) Make up a small quantity of tin glaze (stanniferous or majolica) by adding ten per cent of stannic oxide to standard clear glaze (see Assignment 6).

(2) Glaze the bottle with coloured glaze. Then take an old bristle brush, and flick some of the tin glaze on to the coloured glaze round the upper portion of the bottle, to achieve a gradated effect. When fired, the spattered tin glaze looks like hoar frost. Heavier applications, if required, can be made with a small sponge.

This style of decoration is very attractive if used in conjunction with paper stencils (see Assignment 4).

Fig. 145. The undecorated bottle (left), the turning ring (centre), and the biscuited bottle, glazed and tin-frosted (right).

Assignment 9 – off the Wheel

Pepper and Salt Pots

IN ASSIGNMENT 5, a former was used to shape a simple dish, but its use can be extended to produce other hollow shapes. The former is wrapped round with several layers of newspaper, flat clay is then fitted round this, and the solid former eventually removed. A collection of formers of varying diameters and tapers is useful in any pottery.

DESIGN

Clearly, the shape of the pepper and salt pots must be one that allows the former to be removed. This implies parallel or tapered sides, as opposed to curved ones. However this is not a great restriction, as the sides can be square, round, octagonal, triangular, or a combination of shapes. Work out how the pots are going to be filled. Think about the size of the top of the pots, bearing in mind the number of pour-holes required. Decide whether the top should be flat or canted. If the two pots are to look like one table unit, this must somehow be catered for in your design.

Decide on a final shape and make it up in a solid form – in wood, if you have the necessary skills. If not,

Fig. 147. Two containers designed to take up minimum table space.

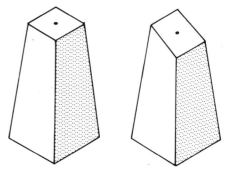

Fig. 148. The top may be either flat or canted.

cast a block of plaster and carve the shape out with a hacksaw or steel scraper, and coarse glasspaper or emery cloth.

WORK SEQUENCE AND DECORATION

(1) Cover the former with three or four layers of newspaper. Do not stick the paper to the former, but fasten the paper to itself with a little Gloy.

(2) Roll out a slab of clay on cartridge paper between $\frac{3}{16}$ in. (5 mm.) ply slats. Wrap this clay round the former so that the sides overlap each other slightly. Make a vertical cut through both pieces of the overlap where they meet half-way. Peel off the top spare piece, then lift the clay a little and remove the bottom spare piece. The two edges will then fit together perfectly. Slip these edges, and model the joint together.

(3) Make the joint good, and smooth it until it is invisible.

(4) Slide out the former. This will leave the paper inside as a lining to hold the pot in shape.

(5) Leave the pot to become leather-hard.

(6) One method of filling the pot is to cut out of the base a hole which can be sealed with a small cork. The cork would prevent the pot from standing straight, so the base is usually fitted a little higher than the bottom of the pot sides.

(7) Cut a card template and fit it in the required base

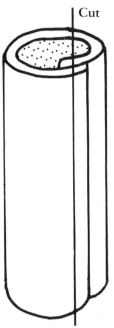

Cut

Fig. 149. Overlapping the clay before cutting ensures a good flush join.

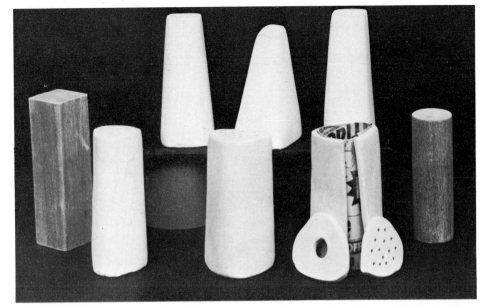

Fig. 151. Stages in forming a pepper pot (foreground), and various formers (background).

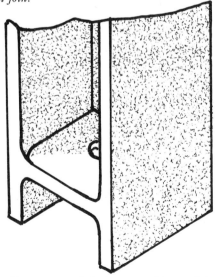

Fig. 150. Arrangement of the base to enable a cork to be fitted.

position. Roll out a small slab of clay, and from it cut a piece the size of the template. When it has hardened, find the centre and cut a hole for the cork with a small knife.

(8) Slip the sides, and insert the circle of clay at the chosen place inside the pot. Lute the edges with a modelling tool, and reinforce them by adding a small roll of clay. If you cannot reach inside with your fingers to support the base during fixing, you may find a piece of wood dowel useful.

(9) Cut out a piece of clay for the top, let it harden, and make the necessary holes. Then slip and lute it in position. Remember that the holes must be large enough to be glazed without clogging.

(10) Clean the pot up, allow it to dry, and biscuit-fire it.

(11) Glaze the pot with an opaque glaze and decorate it by adding a tin frost as described in the on-the-wheel section of this assignment.

63

Assignment 10 – on the Wheel
Hot Water Jug

OBVIOUSLY THIS KIND of jug is not restricted to hot water: it is a basic large jug with a lid, designed to hold hot liquids. A pair of them would be useful, for instance, if you like to serve coffee with hot milk.

DESIGN

A jug in which hot liquids are to be kept needs a lid; this jug, like the lidded pieces in Assignment 5, 6 and 8, has a flange at the top to support the lid. Because of the presence of the flange, the lip will have to be made as in Assignment 8. The lid will probably be on the jug while it is being poured from: some means of preventing the lid from falling off must be devised. One solution is to add a deep flange or collar to the basic thrown lid (see Assignment 6). The deeper the flange, the safer the lid. However this too has to be given thought, since too deep a flange will interrupt the flow of liquid. The immediate answer is a shallow flange. However on reflection it will be clear that a deep flange can in fact be turned to advantage: cut a portion from it at one point for the liquid to flow through; by turning the lid through 90 degrees, slopping can be controlled when the full jug is being carried.

It is a common fallacy that a hole in the lid is cut to let steam escape. In fact it is to allow intake of air, without which pouring would be very difficult. In view of this, you may want to put a hole in the lid of the jug.

The average teacup holds nearly 7 fl. oz. (0.2 litres) of liquid. Pour two cups of water into a jam jar to obtain a rough idea of the size of jug you will need for the quantity of liquid required.

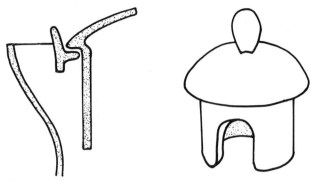

Fig. 152. A deep flange can interrupt the flow of liquid.

Fig. 153. A cut-out in the flange can be useful.

Fig. 154. A badly designed jug.

Form must be related to function when designing a jug. Fig. 154 is an example of a visually pleasing but functionally poor design. You can see what happens when you want to drain the last drops from this jug – it would have to be practically upside down to achieve this. The handle must both look and feel balanced. The lid must suit the overall shape of the jug, and requires a satisfactory grip or knob.

Make some sketches, and cut out the best one in card to see how it looks. Hold it by the handle and tip it as if pouring. It will of course be much lighter than the real thing, but it will give some idea of how the jug will handle.

Fig. 155. Throwing a flanged lid.

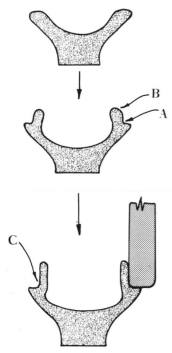

Fig. 156. Stages in throwing a flanged lid.

WORK SEQUENCE

(1) Prepare some clay and divide it into two lumps, one for the pot and one for the lid. These must be made at one and the same time.

(2) Throw the pot, and give it a flange at the top. Trim it, and cut it from the wheel.

(3) Centre the lump of clay for the lid, and begin with a mass in the form of an inverted cone.

(4) In the middle of this throw a small bowl slightly larger than the required size. Lift the sides to make it as even as possible, but keep its rim thick. Try to constrict the portion beneath the bowl as much as possible, since this will reduce the amount of turning required when the knob is formed.

(5) Now make the collar from the thick sides. Let the rim of the bowl run lightly between the finger and thumb of the left hand; with the side of the right thumb partially over the clay, push simultaneously slightly downwards and inwards to produce the result shown at A in Fig. 156.

(6) Raise the thick flange B, which has just been formed, to the required height C. Use callipers to check the diameter of the flange (X on Fig. 157) against the size of the jug top. It should fit loosely, and allowance should be made for glazing; adjustments can easily be made at this stage. If necessary, trim the top level with the needle.

(7) Use a piece of wooden ruler to make the seating angle square, and check the maximum diameter of the lid with the inside flange on the jug (O on Fig. 157). Make allowance for glaze clearance, and correct if necessary. Trim off as much surplus clay as possible with the side tool, and cut the lid from the wheel.

(8) When the jug and lid are leather-hard, they must be turned. The lid can be turned in exactly the same way as the lid in Assignment 6.

(9) Make and fit a wire-pulled handle. A little piece trimmed off the handle will make a small thumb grip, if desired. With a small knife, shape the piece of clay to fit the handle, slip it, and model it on. The grip makes

65

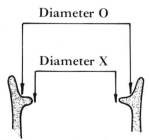

Fig. 157. *Calliper setting when throwing a flanged lid.*

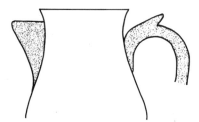

Fig. 158. *Balancing the spout with a thumb grip on the handle.*

the jug easier to handle, and improves its visual line by balancing the spout on the opposite side.

(10) Make a hole in the lid, if desired, with a hole piercer or a small scribing gouge.

DECORATION

This decorative effect is similar to the windows of white slip painted on the mug made in Assignment 1, but it uses a resist agent, a technique that can be used in a number of crafts.

(1) Design a motif based on large areas rather than fine detail. It will be painted on with a brush.

(2) Obtain a small quantity of batik wax, or make up some wax in this way. Put a small tin in a saucepan of water. Place in the tin a small quantity of candle wax diluted with one-third the quantity of paraffin. Heat the saucepan, and stir the wax and paraffin until they are amalgamated and free-flowing. Alternatively, a water-based furniture cream is a serviceable substitute.

(3) Lightly sketch in the window shapes and the brush areas with a pencil or a wooden skewer.

Fig. 159. *Painting a wax resist pattern.*

(4) Paint the brush areas with the hot liquid wax, which will gel immediately on the colder clay.

(5) Paint over the complete window with free-flowing coloured slip. The window edge should either be very clean and crisp, or softened as in Assignment 1.

(6) Leave the jug and the lid to dry thoroughly ready for the biscuit-fire, during which the wax will burn away to expose the pattern areas. Any slip still on the wax before firing will scale off.

(7) Glaze the pot in any transparent glaze.

Assignment 10 —
off the Wheel

Coiled Pot

IMAGINE THE 'MICHELIN MAN' – the well-known symbol of the Michelin Tyre Company – made in clay. This is exactly how a coiled pot is made, each tyre representing a coil of clay.

Although it requires practice to control the shape of a coiled pot well, the technique gives a certain freedom which is not always possible on the wheel. Coiled pots can be made much larger than thrown pots. In some Mediterranean countries and in Africa potters make huge man-sized coiled water-pots. African native women are so skilled at modelling, smoothing, and scraping the built-up layers that the fired pots look as perfect as if they had been thrown on the wheel. When such large pots are being built up, one completed section is left to harden every day to give it rigidity before a new section is added.

Coiling also makes it possible to build rounded shapes that are not based on the circle – asymmetrical pots, oval pots, or pots which turn as they grow.

With such wide scope for design ideas, instructions will be given for coiling in general, rather than for making a specific coiled pot.

DESIGN
For a symmetrical shape, make sketches from which to choose a satisfactory design. Make a full size drawing of this, and from it cut a card template for checking the position of the coils as they are made. In either case a full size card template of the base will be required.

WORK SEQUENCE
When making coiled pots, it is advisable to open the clay a little to facilitate drying, and so minimise the risk of cracking. This involves kneading some grog into a fairly wet sample of clay. Grog is clay which has been biscuited and ground.

There are two methods of building up the wall. Some potters make a long roll of clay, and work round and round in a spiral fashion until the roll is finished; others use one roll for each individual coil. Beginners usually have more success with the second method, which makes it easier to keep the pot rim level and control the shape.

(1) Roll out a flat pancake of grogged clay about $\frac{3}{8}$ in. (10 mm.) thick, put the base template on it, and give it one more roll to anchor it.

(2) Cut out the clay base to the correct size, and place it on a paper-covered flat board. It is essential to make the pot on a rigid base.

(3) Prepare some rolls of grogged clay, each with a diameter of about $\frac{3}{8}$–$\frac{1}{2}$ in. (10–12 mm.) throughout their length, which should be a little more than the circumference of the base. If a wad-box is available, extrude the coils through it using a die of this diameter. Take one of the rolls, and taper one of its ends flat.

(4) Lay this on the clay base, and then wind the roll round the base until the starting-point is reached. Cut any surplus from the end of the roll, and flatten the end to an opposing taper before finally laying it down. The clay coil should now look perfectly level.

(5) Using fingers and a modelling tool, lute this ring well to the base, both inside and outside. Reinforce the inside by modelling-in a narrower clay roll.

(6) Now lay a second roll on top of the first, but start this coil at a different point in the circle to tie in the joint of the first coil. If the pot is to belly out, each coil must overhang the previous one slightly. If each coil sits slightly inside the previous one, the shape will gradually become narrower. For a symmetrical pot, use the template to check the shape after each roll has been laid.

(7) When three or four rolls have been laid, they should be consolidated by stroking and luting together, both inside and outside. Systematic fingering marks can be left, if desired, to give the final pot an interesting

texture. The roll effect may be left on the outside, but inside consolidation is vital, or the pot will emerge from the biscuit-fire as a series of single coils!

(8) After a certain height has been reached, the wall will need to be left to stiffen before adding more coils. Leave the pot in the damp box, or wrapped in polythene, so that it will stiffen but not dry out.

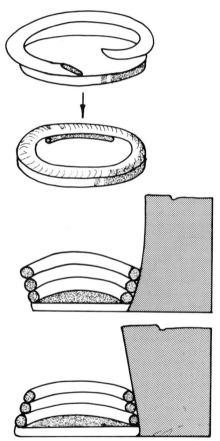

Fig. 160 (top). Fixing the first coil.

Fig. 161 (centre). Strengthening the joint between the first coil and the base with a small roll of clay.

Fig. 162 (bottom). Position of consecutive rolls to cater for different shapes of pot.

Fig. 163. Coiled pot decorated and ready to fire.

DECORATION

(1) Regularly made finger marks can be decorative in themselves, and are an appropriate finish for a hand-built pot. A more regular surface, if preferred, can be achieved by scraping the leather-hard surface with a wooden or plastic scraper, and then burnishing it with the flat surface of the scraper, or an old toothbrush handle. Richer textural effects can be produced by scratching the clay regularly with a metal comb. Raw metallic oxide powders can be rubbed into areas of the clay: on glazing, these create interesting tones.

(2) Allow the vase to dry out slowly, and then biscuit-fire it.

(3) Use any type of suitable glaze.

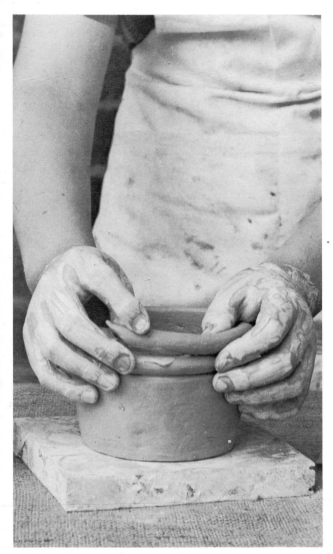

Fig. 164. Making a coiled pot. The first portion has been completed and a coil is shown being added at a later stage.

Assignment 11 – on the Wheel

Large Bottle

THE TECHNIQUE OF gathering-in needs practice, which this piece will provide. It is a larger bottle shape than the one in Assignment 9; the decoration involves cutting areas out of the clay, which makes the bottle very suitable for a table lamp, or a hanging pot to hold a trailing house plant.

DESIGN

Consider first a table lamp. Find out the size of a standard bulb holder, and decide how it is to be fixed: if the bottle is given a flat top, the holder can be glued directly on to this with an epoxy resin glue such as Araldite; if the bottle is left with a hollow top, it can be fitted with a wooden bung to which an adaptor plate has been screwed. Decide where the hole for the cable is to be made. If you are designing a lamp to fit an existing shade, the shape and general proportion of the lamp must be considered in relation to this shade. Sketch both together full size to obtain an idea of the effect. Remember that a lamp needs to be stable.

The plant holder is in fact a plant-pot holder, as the plant itself will be rooted in a thumb pot (see Assignment 1) inside the bottle shape. Decide on a suitable size for the thumb pot, as this obviously has some bearing on the size of the plant holder. Work out a way to hang the plant holder. Think what would be the best place for the pierced holes, so that they show the trailing plant to best advantage. If the thumb pot has a hole underneath like a flower-pot to let excess water drain out, it will collect in the bottom of the plant holder, so the pierced holes should not be too low down. Give some thought to the choice of a glaze colour that enhances, rather than detracts from, a green plant.

69

D

WORK SEQUENCE

(1) Throw the bottle shape in the same way as the small bottle in Assignment 9.

(2) Cut it from the wheel.

(3) When leather-hard, turn the bottle on a suitably-sized ring.

(4) If a top plate with a hole in the centre is to be added, either for fixing the adaptor plate on the table lamp or a string on the plant holder, make a card template so that it can be cut from a rolled out slab. When this plate is leather-hard, slip and lute it on to the bottle.

DECORATION

Table lamp

(1) Design a simple cut-out shape which can be repeated to make an all-over pattern. Cut it out in card, and draw a horizontal centre line on it.

(2) Divide the circumference of the bottle into a number of equal spaces (see Assignment 8), and lightly draw vertical lines through these, using a tri-square.

(3) Decide how many lines of repeat are required horizontally. Space these as desired, and with the aid of a banding-wheel spin guide-lines to mark their position.

(4) Use the card shape to draw the repeat pattern on to the bottle.

(5) Cut the shapes from the bottle with a penknife, and clean up the edges with a small brush.

(6) An interesting and unusual effect can be created by attaching these cut-out shapes with slip, in between the piercings themselves.

(7) When dry, biscuit-fire the lamp.

(8) Apply any suitable glaze.

Plant holder

The piercings here are functional but, as in all good design, try to make them decorative as well. At least one of the holes must be large enough to allow the insertion of the small thumb pot.

(1) Divide the circumference into three, and draw vertical guide-lines.

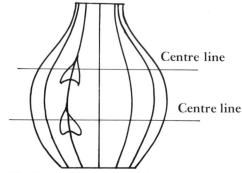

Fig. 165. *Marking positions for piercings.*

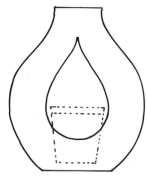

Fig. 166. *The piercings on the plant container must be large enough for a flower pot or thumb pot to be placed inside.*

Fig. 167. *Table lamp base (left), and plant pot (right).*

(2) Cut a card shape (or shapes, if they are not all to be the same size), and draw a vertical centre line on it.

(3) If the piercings are to be symmetrically spaced, select a position on the pot and spin a horizontal line round it.

(4) Mark with the card shape the position of the holes.

(5) Cut out the holes, and clean up the edges.

(6) When dry, biscuit-fire.

(7) Glaze in a colour to suit the plant.

Assignment 11 – off the Wheel
Bulb Pot

THIS TYPE OF BULB pot is usually made in glass. A large bulb, such as a hyacinth, rests in a shaped container at the top of a vase filled with water, which provides nourishment for the roots. This is another example of a composite pot: this time a thumb pot is combined with a shape made on a former. Piercing is again used as a functional decoration.

DESIGN

Measure the widest diameter of a medium-sized hyacinth bulb. Bulb catalogues usually give details of standard graded sizes, which might be helpful. Find out from a gardening book how long the roots are likely to grow.

The tall container for the roots is to be made on a wooden former: design a shape that will be easy to remove. The top portion to hold the bulb is to be made from a thumb pot, suitably pierced. The bulb itself must not be allowed to become soggy and should be well aired, so the pierced decoration will in fact be functional as well as decorative.

The pot and the hyacinth flower will be quite tall, so the pot should be as stable as possible.

WORK SEQUENCE AND DECORATION

(1) Draw the shape full size.

(2) Make up the former in wood or plaster. A wooden former can be planed in a cradle from a suitable-sized block, or turned on a lathe. A plaster former can be cut from a block of plaster cast in a box, and subsequently shaped with a hacksaw or steel scraper, and coarse glasspaper or emery cloth.

71

(3) Coat the former with layers of newspaper, then roll out a slab of clay to cover it. Slip and lute the seam well.

(4) Larger pieces can easily become distorted on removal; to prevent this, stand the former, with its clay cover, upside down on a paper-covered board. The former itself may then be lifted out, and the clay left to dry to leather-hard.

(5) The thumb pot is made exactly as in Assignment 1. Level the top, if necessary, and leave it to dry to leather-hard.

(6) When ready, join both portions together with slip, and model them together.

(7) Cut out the base of the thumb pot, and model the inside to make one continuous open container.

(8) Divide the circumference of the bowl into an equal number of parts.

(9) Cut out a simple shape in card as a template for the piercings.

(10) Draw round the template in each marked space, and then cut out the shapes with a penknife.

(11) Clean up the piercings with a soft brush and a little water.

(12) Leave the pot to dry, and then biscuit-fire it.

(13) Glaze with an opaque, neutral-coloured glaze. Further decoration is superfluous, and would only detract from the hyacinth flower.

Candlesticks can also be made in this way. The thumb pot catches any dripping wax. It is unnecessary to cut away the base of the thumb pot; instead, make an additional ring in which to sit the candle.

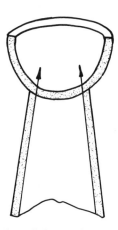

Fig. 169. Section through hyacinth pot to show the portion of clay to be removed.

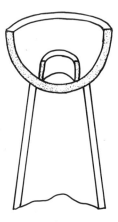

Fig. 170. Section through candlestick.

Fig. 168. Wooden former and components for a composite shape (left), and completed hyacinth pot and candlestick (centre and right).

Assignment 12 – on the Wheel

Water Jug

As in Assignment 11, this jug employs a skill already learnt, but this time using a larger quantity of clay. Centring and clay control are more difficult as larger pots are tackled on the wheel.

A jug for serving water or fruit juice at meals must clearly be larger than the milk jug made in Assignment 3. Since then more practice in shaping has been given, which allows more scope for design.

Two new features are introduced. The jug will not have the customary turned foot, so it must be thrown tidily and cleaned up with the side tool. A new type of handle is used, which is fitted to the jug while still fairly soft. It is known as a pulled handle.

DESIGN

To obtain some idea of the size of jug needed, find out the capacity of the average tumbler or mug. Do not design a shape that is difficult to clean out. The top must be shaped so that it will accommodate a lip. Think carefully about handle shape, size and balance before arriving at the final design, and remember that the jug must be stable.

The outside does not have to be fully glazed, but the inside must be completely glazed to make it waterproof.

WORK SEQUENCE

(1) Throw the jug according to your particular design. Remember to level the top if it finishes a little out of true, and tidy the sides carefully at the bottom where they meet the wheel. Finish by pointing the tool slightly inwards to produce a small bevel.

(2) Pull the lip.

(3) Cut the jug accurately from the wheel with the wire, and set it aside to dry for a little while.

(4) Roll out a thick piece of clay for the handle. Hold it vertically in the left hand, with the fingers curled round the back and the thumb straight across the front.

(5) Wet the roll under a running tap, then wet the right hand and grasp the clay roll in a position exactly opposing that of the left hand.

(6) Move the right hand down the clay roll, pulling and squeezing it very slightly so that fingers and thumb create a suitable shape. Work from front to back, to impart a natural curve. Study Fig. 171 carefully, and then try it out.

The stroking action (not unlike hand-milking a cow!) draws the clay down and makes the roll thinner and longer. Repeat it as many times as necessary, keeping the clay wet, until the roll is a satisfactory size. The handle will become progressively thicker towards the top; this is the most important feature of the pulled handle. The actual cross-section of the handle is controlled by the relative positions of the fingers and thumb of the right hand. The nearer they are together, the flatter the section. The thumb can be kept straight and the fingers well bent to produce a D-shaped cross-section; however if the thumb is turned end-on, a handle with a channel is produced.

(7) Having pulled the handle, pinch off the roll portion by which it was held, and put it aside to dry a little. It must not dry to the leather-hard state, but must still be able to bend under its own weight without cracking.

(8) When the jug is just dry enough to handle safely, lightly roughen and slip the spots to which the top and bottom of the handle are to be attached.

(9) Support the jug with the left index and middle fingers inside and the thumb outside, and press the top end of the handle into position with the right hand, modelling it with the fingers.

(10) Remove the support, and the handle's own weight will make it fall in the form of a natural curve. Give it a slight pull with the right hand, judge the length required, pinch off the surplus, and with the right

73

thumb spring the lower portion on to the slipped area.
(11) Press the handle against the jug, and model with the fingers. Leave the thumb mark, which can look decorative. Tidy the joints if desired, but do not alter the natural curve of the handle.

Some experienced potters attach the roll of clay to the top of the pot before pulling the handle into shape.
(12) Biscuit-fire.

DECORATION

(1) Glaze the inside of the jug with an opaque glaze and dip-glaze the outside, mouth-downwards, so that approximately one-third of the jug is left unglazed.
(2) Depending on the design of the jug, a little relief might help to emphasise its form. Use the sgraffito technique (see Assignment 1) to scratch away not slip this time, but glaze.

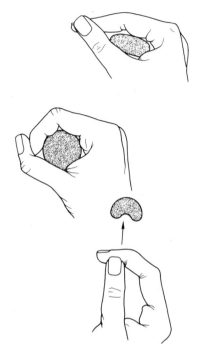

Fig. 171. Pulling a handle.

Fig. 173. Variation in the cross-section of the pulled handle, created by altering the position of the hands.

74

Fig. 172. The decoration must fit the form of the pot (above right).

Fig. 174. Completed jug with a pulled handle.

Assignment 12 –
off the Wheel

Pie Funnel

THE MOULD FOR THE lemon squeezer in Assignment 8 was only capable of casting shapes with a single curve direction. This pie funnel has several curve directions, and therefore requires a different type of mould.

DESIGN

Measure the depth of a typical pie dish to work out a suitable height for the funnel. Steam will form inside the dish as the pie cooks: decide whether the top of the funnel should be enclosed or open. Remember that there will be juice or gravy inside the dish, which may cause suction between the funnel and the bottom of the dish. As always, consider stability, though the funnel must not be so big that there is more funnel than pie in the dish!

Draw a full size sketch and then make a template, first in card and then in tin plate, as for the lemon squeezer. The template should include a small waste portion at the bottom.

WORK SEQUENCE AND DECORATION

(1) Use the same base board and nail as in Assignment 8, but cut out a new plywood disc with the same diameter as the larger end of the funnel.
(2) Model a rough lump of fairly stiff clay on to the ply disc. Make up the form of the pie funnel in this clay, using the tin plate template as a scraper.
(3) Let the clay harden and then remove the shape from the plywood.
(4) Mark two diametrically opposite points on the clay base, and then make two vertical guide-lines with a tri-square to divide the clay mass in half.
(5) The plaster mould must be made in two halves, each corresponding to half the clay mass. Fig. 179 shows how the mould is cast.

Lay the clay model horizontally in a block of soft clay, and bury it up to the dividing line. The waste end of the model should be left free on the outside; one side of the casting-box will rest against this.
(6) Surround the assembly with a casting-box, and seal all the joints with clay to prevent leakage of plaster.
(7) Mix sufficient plaster to fill the casting-box to a depth of about $1\frac{3}{4}$ in. (40 mm.) above the clay model.
(8) When the plaster has set, remove the box and the block of soft clay. This leaves the clay model half buried in plaster.
(9) The two plaster halves must register accurately – use the handle of a teaspoon to cut dome-shaped knatch holes at each of the four plaster corners.
(10) Soap-size the plaster surface and the sides.
(11) Put the casting-box back, seal it, and pour the plaster to make the second half of the mould.
(12) When the plaster is dry, remove the casting-box, separate the two halves of the mould, and remove the clay model.
(13) When the plaster mould has fully dried, tie the two halves together, either with string or with heavy-duty rubber bands, and fill the mould with defloccu-lated clay slip. Pour out the surplus slip after about twenty minutes.
(14) Allow enough time for the cast to harden before opening the mould, or the cast will sag. The clay will have shrunk during preliminary drying, and can easily be removed from the plaster cast.
(15) Fig. 177 shows how the pie funnel will look when it is removed. The waste rim must now be removed, and a hole must be cut in the top to allow steam to escape.
(16) Three or four pieces should be cut away from the base to allow juices to enter. Divide the circumference into three or four sections, and cut a card template the shape of the piece to be removed. Then mark the

pieces and cut them out with a small damp knife.

(17) Clean the funnel with the sponge, and leave it to dry ready for the biscuit-fire.

(18) Use any suitable glaze.

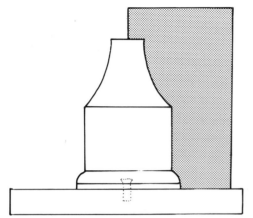

Fig. 175. *Jig and template for forming the pie funnel 'blank'.*

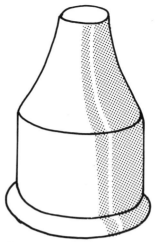

Fig. 177. *Pie funnel as cast.*

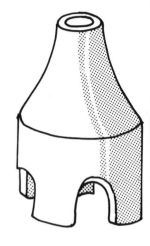

Fig. 178. *Pie funnel with the waste rim removed, the top pierced, and the base crenellated.*

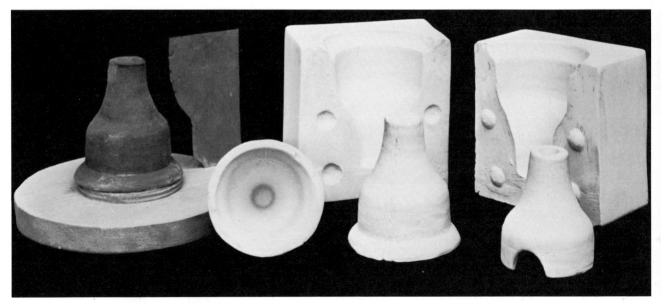

Fig. 176. *Making a pie funnel: forming the initial solid model* (left), *the two halves of the mould* (background), *two views of the funnel as cast* (centre), *and the completed funnel* (right).

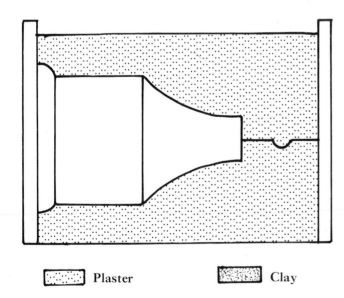

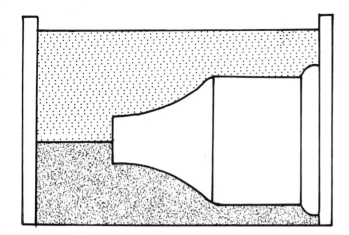

| Plaster | | Clay |

Fig. 179. Making the pie funnel mould.

Assignment *13 –* on the Wheel

Fruit Salad Bowl

THIS BOWL IS BASICALLY the same as the one in Assignment 4, but, as it is larger, more clay must be manipulated.

DESIGN

Remember that the inside of a bowl should have a true curve, whether shallow or steep. Do not make the bowl too large at this stage; the maximum diameter should not be more than about $8\frac{1}{2}$ in. (204 mm.). Make sketches of its section to indicate shape.

As before, consider certain functional details: the bowl will contain a considerable amount of liquid; a large spoon will be dipped into it; and it will have to be carried from the kitchen. With these factors in mind, decide whether a shallow or a deep bowl would be better. Work out how the shape of the bowl can help to reduce possible slopping while being carried, and at the table.

WORK SEQUENCE

(1) Throw the bowl in the same way as the small bowl in Assignment 4, but first consider how to use the clay. A larger diameter bowl requires a much thicker top wall to be left at the end of the lifting movement, so that enough clay remains for the rim to be stretched to the required size.

(2) When the bowl is leather-hard, turn the foot. Glazing the outside will be much easier if the base profile is finished in such a way that it acts as a finger grip.

(3) Biscuit-fire the bowl when dry.

DECORATION

Under-glaze colours have already been used, ground with a siccative, for painting on to biscuit. These colours are also available in the form of crayon sticks, which will be used for decorating this bowl.

One or two problems will be encountered with this method of decoration. The sticks are sometimes square and awkward to point, so it is often difficult to know exactly where on the pot the mark will be made. The sticks are also very brittle and crack easily. If the biscuit is very rough, the colours bite too easily, wear away quickly and leave a somewhat patchy line. Finally, as the sticks have no siccative, glazing must be carried out very carefully. However do not be discouraged from using crayons, for a crayon-decorated pot is rarely seen and the variation in texture is very attractive.

(1) Rough-in the design on the biscuit – this will burn away in the glaze fire – and then complete it with crayons. Take great care not to smudge the work as you are doing it. It is wise to work from the centre of the bowl outwards, though if you have designed a complete picture rather than just random motifs this may not always be possible.

(2) Glaze is best sprayed on to crayon-decorated pots, if facilities are available, to prevent the colour running. Use a transparent glaze to let the crayon decoration show through.

Fig. 181. Bowl decorated with under-glaze crayons, ready for glazing.

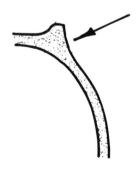

Fig. 180. Turning a grip on the foot of a bowl.

Assignment 13 – off the Wheel

Tiles

MAKING CERAMIC TILES is very rewarding – they have many uses, can be produced from a variety of clays, and many decorative techniques can be used on them. Tiles can be cut with a wire from a block of clay, formed in a mould, or cut from a rolled out piece of clay. A single tile, backed with felt, makes an excellent teapot- or kettle-stand. A few hand-made decorative tiles interspersed with plain mass-produced ones can add a touch of individuality to a kitchen or bathroom. The craft of pottery can be combined with woodwork to produce cheese boards and small tables and trays incorporating tiles in their design. Chess table tops with small clay tiles in two tones can serve a dual purpose – when not being used for playing chess, drinks or coffee can be served on them.

DESIGN

The pattern needs careful consideration; bear in mind how and where the tiles are to be used. Each tile can be a unit in itself, or it can be considered as one of a number, the full effect of the pattern being seen only when the tiles are mounted. The design considerations are similar to those involved when designing a unit for fabric printing. Considerable scope is possible in the treatment: decoration can be geometric (paper stencils, as used in Assignment 4, could be used), abstract, or pictorial.

The size of the tiles will be closely linked with the style of pattern, and their intended use: 4½ in. (113 mm.) square and ½ in. (12 mm.) thick is a good general size. Remember that a tile shrinks, when made, by about one-tenth or one-twelfth. If the tiles are to be used to form a composite decoration or surface, it is important that each tile should be perfectly square.

Fig. 182. Tile designs can be made which are complete in themselves but which, when regrouped, make larger design units.

Of all the many styles open to the tile maker, one of the most interesting is an inlay pattern. This technique was used by Cistercian monks in medieval times for making floor tiles in the abbeys then being built. Tiles found at Ely and Chester Cathedrals and Westminster Abbey are excellent examples of their craft. The procedure involved making recesses with a wooden die in a red earthenware tile; these recesses were then filled with a white clay. From the design point of view, these encaustic tiles, as they are called, served their purpose well, since wear did not affect the pattern. Medieval tiles offer a wealth of inspiration for patterns: some are geometric, others heraldic; some depict landscapes and others flowers.

Study some of these tiles if possible – local churches can often provide examples. Failing this, the local public library will probably have books with illustrations of them. Then design your own tile on paper. As a beginner, concentrate on balance and avoid too many intricacies.

79

WORK SEQUENCE AND DECORATION

One of the chief problems when making ceramic tiles is that of warping. A tile made in any of the common clays will be far from flat when dry. In industry the problem is largely overcome by making tiles which need no drying out; they are in fact dust-pressed, so no shrinkage occurs. It is impossible to guarantee flatness in hand-made tiles, but warping can be minimised by adding a quantity of grog to the body, and by careful stacking and drying.

(1) Roll out a slab of clay on a piece of cartridge paper between $\frac{1}{2}$ in. (12 mm.) slats, and when leather-hard cut from it an accurate square tile. Also roll out between slats a slab of clay $\frac{1}{8}$ in. (3 mm.) thick, and let this become leather-hard too.

(2) Place the design on the tile, and trace the pattern through lightly with a sharp hard pencil.

(3) Now remove the paper cartoon and cut out with scissors the individual shapes, which are later to be filled with a different coloured clay. If the pattern is symmetrical and the shapes are regularly repeated, only one of each need be cut out.

(4) From the thin slab of clay cut out the required number of shapes to build up the pattern, using the paper cut-outs as templates.

(5) With a little slip, stick these pieces in the right places on the tile, and press them well down.

(6) With a modelling tool or small knife, lightly taper the edges of the raised pieces towards the top.

(7) Make a small casting-box into which the tile will fit accurately. Four pieces of wood tacked together will serve the purpose well.

(8) Seal all the joints with clay on the outside of the box, and place it on a level surface. Mix and pour in enough plaster to cover the clay to a depth of about $\frac{5}{8}$ in. (15 mm.).

(9) When the plaster is set, remove the box and the clay so that a slab of plaster remains, with the pattern on its surface in the form of hollows. Rub the flat side

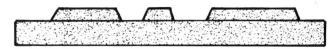

Fig. 183. The edges of the raised portions must be tapered to allow for casting.

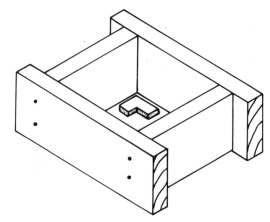

Fig. 184. Casting-box with modelled tile in position, ready for the plaster pour.

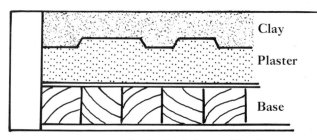

Clay

Plaster

Base

Fig. 185. Determining the depth of the moulding-box.

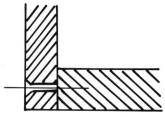

Fig. 186. Screwing on the sides of the box in which the tiles are to be moulded.

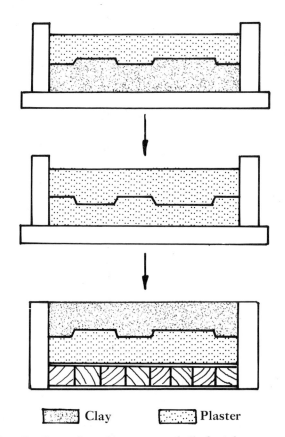

Clay   **Plaster**

Fig. 187. Stages in making a recessed tile for inlay decoration.

of the plaster on a sheet of abrasive paper to remove any irregularities.

(10) After a short period of drying, soap-size this cast slab on the pattern side and on all four edges, replace it in the casting-box, re-seal, and pour another layer of plaster about $\frac{5}{8}$ in. (15 mm.) deep.

(11) When the twinned plaster has become hard, plunge it into a bowl of water. It will then be possible to separate the two matching layers. One will be an exact replica of the original clay model. True the reverse side of this, as before, on a sheet of abrasive paper.

(12) Leave the casts to dry (this will take a few days). Check on flatness, squareness, and regularity of thickness. Any irregularities at this stage can be removed with glasspaper.

(13) Now make a wooden moulding-box similar to the casting-box previously constructed, but more accurate in depth.

Cut a piece of blockboard or thin ply to the exact size of the plaster. Plane a piece of $\frac{3}{8}$ in. (10 mm.) softwood five times as long as the side of the tile; the width is worked out by adding together the thickness of the blockboard or ply; the thickness of the cast minus the raised portions; and the thickness of the final tiles minus $\frac{1}{2}$ in. (12 mm.). From the length of timber, cut two pieces exactly equal in length to the side of the tile, and divide the remaining wood into two equal lengths. Drill and countersink screw holes along the lower edge of each piece, in an appropriate position for screwing to the base. Screw on with 1 in. (24 mm.) no. 6 screws the two pieces which are the exact length of the side of the tile. A bradawl will help to get the screws started. Finally, fix the two remaining pieces, allowing an equal overhang at each end.

(14) Place the cast carrying the raised portions in the moulding-box. Fill it with small pieces of grogged red clay and press them well down. Great care must be taken to ensure a clean pressing, and to avoid creating small air pockets. Over-fill the box slightly, and level the top by striping with a damp ruler.

(15) After about half an hour, the dry plaster will have absorbed some of the moisture from the clay. Loosen the screws holding the sides to allow the cast plus cast tile to tip out. It will then be possible to separate the two.

(16) Paint the hollows in the clay tile with white slip, and fill them with small pieces of grogged white clay, pressing them well down as before. Level the tile roughly with a damp ruler, and then put it aside to dry. Tiles are best dried on a flat wire mesh (like the ones used in kitchens for cooling cakes). This allows air circulation and minimises warping.

81

(17) When completely dry, rub the tile on a sheet of abrasive paper to make the pattern show up clearly.

(18) If tiles are to be mounted as a composite piece, they are glazed on the pattern side only, but if a single tile is required, the edges are glazed also. If used as a table stand, the reverse side should be covered with a layer of baize or felt.

Any number of tiles can be similarly made, and each will be identical in pattern and size. The plaster cast takes on the rôle of the wooden die which was used by the monks.

Now consider some of the possibilities for variations on this technique. The clays could, for instance, be reversed so that the white was filled with red. Instead of using the final plaster cast, the waste mould can be used, and tiles with a raised decoration produced in the moulding-box. Metallic oxides can be used to stain the white clay used for filling, thus producing a variety of coloured inlays. The recesses in the tiles can be filled with pools of coloured glaze to produce a similar effect to *cloisonné* enamelling. Alternatively they can be filled with powdered glass (cullet), since tile surfaces, unlike the side of a pot, can be kept flat during firing and the molten glass will not run off. In this way bright reds and oranges are possible. Cullet requires a low fire of about 700°C.

Fig. 188. Making inlaid tiles.

Figs. 189–90. Making raised tiles.

Assignment 14 – on the Wheel

Biscuit Barrel

THE LAST THREE assignments have concentrated on providing experience in making larger versions of pot forms introduced earlier in the book. A larger bottle, a larger jug, and a larger bowl have been made. In each case, some new feature was also included. To round off this sequence, a larger covered pot should now be attempted.

If you have access to a kiln that can achieve stoneware temperatures, it will be possible to make a casserole. If limited to earthenware, similar practice can be provided by making what is often still called a biscuit 'barrel', since traditionally it has assumed the wooden barrel form.

DESIGN

It must be possible to take a biscuit from the barrel, so the opening must be large enough for a hand. The question of storage is important, since biscuits go soft if not properly covered. The very large opening which makes it easy to get biscuits out is not as good from the point of view of air-tightness, and a compromise is perhaps inevitable. Biscuits vary tremendously in size, so plan the size of your barrel with a large biscuit in mind. A $\frac{1}{2}$ lb. (226 g.) packet of large biscuits will provide a rough idea of how much space will be necessary to store this quantity.

Decide on a suitable type of lid. A handle or handles might be useful, but a jug-type handle would hardly look right. Consider some alternative handle forms that are more appropriate.

Make some sketches of various shapes, and choose the best one as a design.

WORK SEQUENCE

(1) Throw the pot in the usual way, keeping the wall farily thick at the top in order to produce a flange.
(2) Throw the lid to fit, checking the size with callipers.
(3) Set both pot and lid aside to dry and, when ready, turn them in the usual way.
(4) Suitable handles can be made in a number of ways. A woven cane handle combines the crafts of basketry and pottery, and would do very well. It requires a clay lug on each side of the barrel, through which to bend the slivered cane.
(5) Another solution is to provide side handles. It is useful to know how to make these, as they can be used on many other containers. Fig. 191 shows a section through pick-up handles; the elevation forms part of a circle. To make the handles, throw a ring on the wheel – the walls should be of the required thickness and the circumference should provide the correct elevation curvature.
(6) Cut the ring from the wheel and allow it to dry to leather-hard.
(7) From the ring, cut handles of the required size – they can be short arcs or complete semi-circles, according to preference.
(8) If the barrel has curved sides, trim the back of the handles to fit the curvature of the pot in both plan and elevation (A and B respectively in Fig. 193).
(9) Fix the handles with slip at diametrically opposite positions, and lute them with the modelling tool.

DECORATION

A textural effect can be created on the side handles described above, by throwing a moulding on the outside of the ring, or by modelling flutes or reeds in the top curved surface.

The barrel itself is to be decorated using the glaze-on-glaze technique. Practise making good clean strokes on old newspaper – use a large sable-hair brush, well charged with powder or watercolour. Then sketch on the newspaper the shape of the biscuit barrel, and see if

83

its form can be emphasised with two or three bold brush strokes. Keep making trials on the newspaper until one of them seems right, and you feel that you can make the required brush strokes deftly.

(1) Glaze the barrel in an opaque glaze.

(2) When it has dried, make the brush strokes on top of this glaze, charging the brush with glaze of a contrasting colour. Decorate in this way either on one side only, or repeated at a number of points on the barrel.

In many ways this is similar to the technique of majolica painting in Assignment 6.

Fig. 191. Section through the thrown ring from which side handles are to be cut.

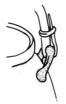

Fig. 192. Clay lugs must be fitted for a cane handle.

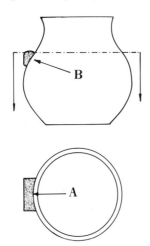

Fig. 193. Profiles to be considered when fitting side handles.

Fig. 194. Side handles may be decorated by fluting.

Fig. 195. Simple brush stroke decoration is suitable for the biscuit barrel.

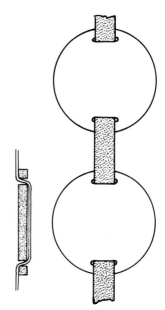

Fig. 196. Hanging units can be threaded on a strap for display.

Assignment 14 — off the Wheel

Wall Hanging

SUCCESS IN ART AND craft practice is very closely connected with suitability for purpose. Some objects and shapes are feasible if made in metal, but would be quite impractical if made in wood. Some can be fabricated quite happily in clay, while others are better conceived in glass. The concept also applies to decorative work, especially in ceramics.

This wall hanging makes use of a number of decorative techniques previously encountered.

DESIGN

The hanging will consist of a number of repeat units with various decorative embellishments, strung one above the other like horse brasses. The decoration on the individual units might include piercing, underglaze or majolica painting, sgraffito and relief.

Before starting work, a number of questions must be considered. There is an obvious limit to the size of each unit, both vertically and horizontally. Think about the number of units to be included in the complete decorative piece – the length of the hanging will be influenced by the height of each unit, and the number of units strung together. Decide whether the units are to be round, square, hexagonal, octagonal, oval, or of indefinite shape. They can have a common decorative theme, or they can be unified solely by their common shape and size.

Consider how they are to be hung. They might be stuck with a strong adhesive such as Araldite to a strip of hessian, felt, or leather. They could be threaded on a strap – this involves cutting slots, which would have to be incorporated into the decorative scheme. Each individual unit could be hung, in brace button fashion, to a wide leather strap (a single slot would probably have to be cut in each unit). If holes were cut in appropriate places, the units could be strung one to the other with coloured cord.

Work out your ideas on paper using a suitable medium. It is no use trying to design a brush pattern with a pencil, or using a paintbrush for a pattern which is going to be scratched. Designs for piercing and relief modelling must be considered specifically in relation to clay as a medium. Imagine two units to be decorated by piercing, one in clay and one in metal. The metal is much harder and far less brittle at the working stage, and a little consideration will make it abundantly clear that, when working in clay, the spaces between the pierced areas must be much larger in order to prevent one pierced area breaking into the next. Sufficient clay must also be left between the outer pierced areas and the edge of the piece itself. Such limiting factors do not apply when making a relief pattern, where raised areas may be suitably linked if necessary.

WORK SEQUENCE AND DECORATION

(1) Make several identical card templates.

(2) Roll out a slab of white clay between $\frac{5}{16}$ in. (8 mm.) slats.

(3) Using one of the templates, cut out one unit shape. Clean it up well, and leave it to dry ready for the biscuit-fire. It will subsequently be painted with an underglaze pattern.

(4) If a majolica-painted unit is to be included, treat a second clay shape in the same way.

(5) Cut out one more unit shape from the clay slab, coat it with a layer of contrasting coloured slip, allow it to harden a little, and then work a sgraffito pattern through the slip layer.

In the three cases above, remember to make any necessary fixing holes or slots.

(6) Draw the chosen design for piercing on another of the card templates, and cut out the pattern as if cutting

85

a stencil. Place the template on the rolled out clay between the slats, and give the clay a further light roll. This will transfer an impression of the design to the clay.

(7) Cut out the unit as before, and put it aside to dry. When leather-hard, cut out the pattern with a small knife and soften the edges with a damp squirrel-hair brush or sponge.

(8) If more than one unit is required with relief decoration, model one, and then take a plaster cast.

(9) Cut out one more basic clay unit, and on this trace the outline of the relief pattern. Build this up in clay, adopting the method used for encaustic tiles. Additional detail and varying levels of relief can be modelled into or on to the main raised areas.

Having completed the modelling, cut a strip of clay about 1 in. (24 mm.) wide from a rolled out slab of clay, and use it to erect a cottle round the modelled shape. Lute the wall to the clay base on the underside, making sure, as usual, that the joint in the wall is sealed. Mix and pour a little plaster, which, when set, will form a reverse of the relief decoration.

To make the actual units, press sufficient clay on to this to fill the recesses and stand $\frac{5}{16}$ in. (7 mm.) proud. Trim the clay edges against the plaster and make sure the top is level. Make the necessary slots or holes for hanging purposes.

(10) Make any further units required for the hanging, and vary their treatment, using any or all of the decorative techniques already practised. Interest will be provided by variety and contrast. The painted units should have clear or majolica glazes, the sgraffito one can be left in its natural colour or glazed with a transparent coloured glaze, and the remaining pieces glazed in any opaque glaze. This is an opportunity to use up remaining small quantities of glaze, or a sample made up for trials.

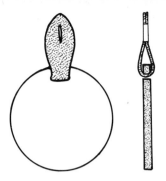

Fig. 197. Fixing hanging units to a strap, brace fashion.

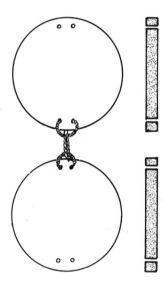

Fig. 198. Hanging units linked with string.

Fig. 199. Parts of a relief pattern can be freely linked.

Fig. 200. *Biscuit barrel before decoration, together with the thrown ring and the handle cut from it.*

Fig. 201. *Units for a wall hanging, decorated with sgraffito, piercing and under-glaze painting (foreground), and stages in making a relief unit (background).*

Assignment 15 – on the Wheel

Pots Inspired by Natural Shapes

IN ALL THE WORK so far, a particular objective has been aimed at – a modelled animal, for instance, or a jug with a lid. Within these limits, there has been a certain amount of freedom of choice based on personal selection of shape, size, and decoration. A considerable amount of information about materials, decorative methods, and techniques should have been acquired. Now use this knowledge and exercise your imagination in a more ambitious project, whose terms of reference are not so clearly defined.

In Assignment 2 the great variety of shapes found in beach pebbles was suggested as inspiration for pot forms. Look at natural shapes again to find inspiration for a pot or group of pots to be made on the wheel. A work sequence will not be provided as it would not be common to every pot.

One or two examples of natural shapes on which pot designs could be based might be helpful. Examine some pumpkins and ornamental gourds, or study the shape of the fruits and seed heads of roses and poppies. Watch water or thick oil dripping slowly from a tube. Sketch the shapes you see forming during the process, and then use these shapes as the basis for a set of bottle vases. It is a good idea to keep a sketch book and record in it interesting shapes. Some will inspire work on the wheel, others will suggest pots of a more irregular nature – hand-built pots and ornaments which are designed purely for visual enjoyment.

Fig. 202. Set of pots inspired by watching oil falling from a dropper.

Assignment 15 – off the Wheel

Ash Tray

IN ASSIGNMENT 7 A sugar basin was made from one piece of clay by the method known as development. There is also another method of using slabs of clay to form shapes: flat slabs of clay are cut to size, slipped and luted together.

Many useful and decorative articles can be made in this way, such as money boxes, ash trays, cheese boards, and stands for hot casseroles or teapots. These pieces are enhanced by a stamped-in decoration. This style of decorating was used on a simple scale in Assignment 2, where the area between the rolls was textured. Instead of using random objects as stamps, make your own stamps in plaster of Paris.

DESIGN

If making a money box, measure the largest coin in circulation to determine the right size for the coin slot. Decide on a method by which the money can be taken out when required. Think about shape – does a money box always have to be rectangular? It could, for instance, be cylindrical. Decide which surface would be best decorated with stamps.

Many ash trays tend to tip over far too easily: work out how to prevent this. If the ash bowl is too small and shallow, ash tends to spread on to the surrounding table area; decide on an adequate size and shape. The design should incorporate an area (possibly cigarette-shaped) on which to rest a lighted cigarette. Think what is the most attractive way of using the plaster stamps on the ash tray. One solution to all these design considerations is shown in Fig. 211, but there are many others equally good.

Fig. 203. Stylus for making stamped-in decoration.

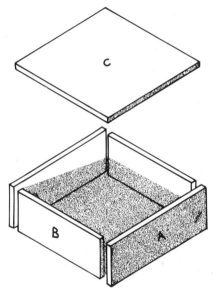

Fig. 204. Templates are required for the sides and base.

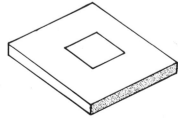

Fig. 205. Size of the stamp marked on the clay slab.

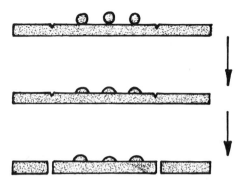

Fig. 206. Building up the original relief pattern for making a plaster stamp.

Fig. 207. Making a plaster stamp (left), and some examples of stamps (right).

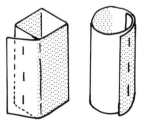

Fig. 208. Stapling together the card cottles for casting the stamps.

89

WORK SEQUENCE AND DECORATION

Instructions are given here for an ash tray, but the basic procedure is the same for any slab-built piece.

(1) Using a drawing board, T square and set square, draw and cut card templates for the individual components. For the ash tray illustrated, they comprise a template for the long sides (A), a template for the short sides (B), and a template for the top (C). One slab must always overlap the other, so that if a square is required the two short sides must be shorter than the long sides by twice the thickness of the clay slabs. The top must be large enough to overlap all the sides.

(2) The shape of the plaster stamp should fit the shape of the area in which it is to be used – in this case it is right-angled. It is best, too, if the stamp leaves a good border round the area decorated by it – the corners can then be luted without damaging the pattern.

(3) Roll out a small piece of clay about $2\frac{5}{8}$ in. (60 mm.) square, and about $\frac{3}{8}$ in. (10 mm.) in thickness. Mark on it the size and shape of the stamp.

(4) Make some tiny rolls of clay and arrange them within this area to form an interesting pattern, which should be kept as simple as possible. Lightly press the rolls on to the clay base with the fingers.

(5) Let the whole piece dry to leather-hard, and then use a small modelling tool or sharpened piece of wood (a whittled-down lollipop stick is ideal) to model the rolls to a semi-circular cross-section in order to eliminate any undercuts.

(6) Finish the surface with a soft brush dipped in water, to remove any tool marks.

(7) When complete, cut the modelled shape from the slab of clay with a damp knife.

(8) Make a card wall about 3 in. (75 mm.) high for this shape, giving the joint a very generous overlap. The joint itself can easily be made with a stapler.

(9) Roll out a fairly thick pancake of soft clay; place the modelled piece on this, and surround it with the white card wall which should fit snugly against it. Press the card lightly into the soft clay to create a plaster seal at the base.

(10) Mix a little plaster of Paris. It should be slightly thicker than that used for casting – about 7 oz. (200 g.) of plaster to 5 fl. oz. (0.15 litres) of water – and when ready, pour it into the card mould. Tap the work surface to make sure that no air bubbles are trapped within the modelled space.

(11) When the plaster is set, peel off the card and remove the initial clay pattern to reveal a plaster stamp which is the exact reverse of the one originally modelled. Allow the stamp to become really hard.

(12) Roll out some clay into a large slab about $12\frac{1}{2}$ in. $\times$ $8\frac{1}{2}$ in. $\times$ $\frac{3}{16}$ in. thick (300 mm. $\times$ 200 mm. $\times$ 5 mm.). From it cut four pieces: two should be a little larger than template A and two a little larger than template B.

(13) Impress the stamp into the four pieces of clay to make an attractive set of imprints. The pressure of the stamp will inevitably cause an uneven edge to form. For this reason the development method is not used in conjunction with stamped decoration.

(14) Return the four slabs to correct template size by cutting away the surface with a damp knife. It is helpful to draw lines to mark the centre of the template both vertically and horizontally. This will aid correct positioning in relation to the stamped pattern.

(15) Roll out another slab, and cut a piece for the top, to the size of template C.

(16) Make the ash bowl as a thumb pot, and link it to the top slab in the same way as the pot in Assignment 1.

(17) Set aside all five parts until they are leather-hard, turning them over periodically to ensure flatness during the initial drying stage.

(18) To assemble the ash tray, slip and lute together one short and one long side. Repeat the process to join the remaining two sides. Lute both these pairs together, resting the bottom edges on a flat surface covered with cartridge paper. Check for alignment. Slip and model-on the top. Trim off any irregular edges, and complete by sponging the piece lightly all over.

(19) Set the ash tray aside to dry slowly for the biscuit-fire.

(20) After biscuiting, glaze with any suitable opaque coloured glaze.

(21) It is a good idea to glue strips of baize or felt to the bottom edges of the ash tray. It can then be safely placed on polished surfaces without scratching them – but remember not to immerse the ash tray completely when it is washed.

Fig. 211. *Money box, rectangular vase, and ash tray.*

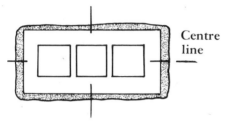

Centre line

Fig. 209. *The decorative border must be central on each side.*

Fig. 210. *Components of a slab-built ash tray.*

Assignment 16 – on the Wheel

Teapot

A TEAPOT IS USUALLY considered a difficult exercise, but it need not be, provided a few elementary design rules are followed.

Teapots are composite pieces – a covered pot, fitted with a spout and handle – and can be made in a variety of ways. Commercially produced teapots are cast in plaster of Paris moulds, separate moulds being made for the pot, the lid, the spout, and the handle. Making a set of these moulds is a more advanced task, but there is no reason why some parts, especially the spout, should not be cast in a small pottery if it is impossible to make them satisfactorily any other way.

DESIGN

In Assignment 10 it was necessary to work out the size of pot required to hold two teacups of liquid. This information should be helpful in working out a suitable size for the teapot. Fill the teapot at home with water. See how many cups can be filled from it, and co-ordinate the result with the height and width of the teapot. You will probably find that your original ideas about size were far too large – the size of a teapot in relation to its capacity can be very deceptive.

Since the teapot is to be thrown, do not design a shape that will be difficult to throw – remember that many of the shapes bought in shops are not thrown, but cast. Think about what effect shape might have on the rate at which the teapot cools.

The top of the spout must be at the same height as the teapot top; otherwise tea will spill out when the pot is full. The angle and shape of the spout will affect how the pot pours – if the spout is too straight, there will be a sudden rush of liquid. The actual pouring end of the spout is really a lip, and therefore requires a double curve (see Assignment 3). If tea-bags are to be used, a straight exit hole to the spout is all that is required; otherwise straining holes will be required to prevent loose tea leaves being poured into the cups along with the liquid. Remember that the spout will form part of a visual whole, so shape, size, and lines should all harmonise with the pot itself.

When designing the lid, bear in mind that the pot has to be tipped to pour out the tea. As with the spout, give some thought to the overall shape of the finished teapot. The lid should follow the general line of the body of the pot, and the knob should reflect the body shape. The knob must provide a good grip, since the lid will be hot. The question of a hole in the lid was considered when the hot water jug in Assignment 10 was being designed. Remember that the teapot must be regularly emptied and washed; a fairly large mouth is required.

The handle must provide a good hold, as the pot will be reasonably heavy when full, and it should be placed where it will give good balance when pouring. Like the lid and spout, it should be in keeping with the general shape of the pot.

The most difficult task when sketching shapes is to achieve good visual balance between the projecting spout and the projecting handle – a thumb grip, or a handle which is not part of a complete curve, can often help.

Consider all these points carefully, and then make sketches to help formulate your ideas. Make a final choice, and then draw a full size section of it. Cut out the complete pot shape in card, to see how well it handles.

WORK SEQUENCE

(1) Much will depend upon final design, but in any case start by throwing the body of the pot to the size and shape of the cut-out. An inside template is useful

for checking. Make a flange at the top to contain the lid.

(2) Throw the lid, and make a collar (see Assignment 10).

(3) The spout can be thrown, shaped in a former, or cast in a two-part mould. Instructions are given for all three methods. Whichever method is used, both the spout and the lid must be leather-hard before they are joined.

If the spout is in the form of a bent cone, it can be thrown on the wheel, but presents a problem: it will not be large enough to get the left hand inside. Centre a small piece of clay, and leave it in the form of a fairly tall narrow cylinder.

(4) Open it out with the right thumb. It is best to leave a base, which will help to retain the spout shape and can be cut off later.

(5) Raise the wall to a tall taper, using the first and second fingers of the left hand inside, and squeezing rather more with the right hand than with the left.

(6) Gather-in the shape, using the six-point constricting movement described and illustrated in Assignment 9.

(7) Probably not even a single finger will fit inside for the final shaping of the spout end. Solve this problem by holding inside a small piece of dowel rod or the handle of a large watercolour brush. Throw against this with the right hand.

(8) Put the fingers and palm of the right hand round the spout, and carefully bend it over. Try not to distort its rotundity.

(9) Cut the spout off with the wire. An experienced potter usually throws the spout on top of a larger piece of clay. When the spout is complete, he cuts it from the main mass with a needle while the wheel is still spinning, holding the spout gently with his left hand.

(10) If you are not yet confident enough to throw a spout, make one round a turned wooden former (see Assignment 9). The bend can be made while the clay is still plastic, in a similar way to the thrown spout.

(11) If the design does not make a thrown or formed spout feasible, cast it in a two-part plaster mould. Wait until the pot is leather-hard, and then cut out two pieces of card to the required shape of the spout, and fit the ends of these exactly to the pot in the correct position.

(12) On one piece model half a spout in clay. Remember that it will become gradually thicker towards its base, and that the clay being modelled represents the external size of the spout.

(13) Model an equal section on the reverse side of the other piece of card.

(14) Peel off the card from each, and join the two halves together with a little slip; this is an easier method than trying to model a complete spout. A little extra modelling here and there will be needed to make the spout symmetrically correct.

(15) Fit the solid spout against the pot, and adapt the end of the spout to the round form of its profile. In most cases, a little extra clay will have to be modelled-on to achieve this.

(16) Add to the lip end a small cone of clay, which will serve as a slip reservoir, and add to the end which will fit against the body of the pot a larger, tapered, solid piece of clay. In both cases, the smaller diameter of the tapered extra clay should be equal to the internal size of the spout. Be quite sure that the ledges formed at each end are not undercut, which would make it difficult to remove them from the mould. The large piece of clay added to the pot end of the spout will serve as a pouring gate.

(17) Make a two-piece mould from this model (see Assignment 12). The half-way line corresponds to the junction of the two original halves. The clay forming the pouring plug will, of necessity, have to be flush with the side of the casting-box.

(18) Allow the mould to dry, and then pour in some deflocculated slip; let it stand for about ten minutes, and then pour the slip out. When the mould is opened, the hollow spout will be practically ready for use. Cut away the base end, remove the cone at the lip, and clean the spout up.

(19) Turn a foot on the pot, and turn a knob on the lid.

(20) The handle can be wire-cut or pulled, depending on the design. If the handle requires a sudden change in direction, coax it carefully on the paper to avoid cracking. When made, let it dry, like the spout, to leather-hard.

(21) Assemble the pieces of the teapot as follows. If the spout has been thrown or made on a former, cut it off to the correct length and shape to fit the profile of the pot. A moulded spout obviously needs no further trimming.

(22) When it fits well, hold the spout in position on the body of the pot and draw round it with a sharp pencil. Remember to leave enough space inside this mark for the thickness of the spout itself, and within these limits either cut out a complete hole, or cut perforations with a hole piercer.

(23) Coat the surface with slip, press spout and pot firmly together and lute the join with the modelling tool. Pay particular attention to the mouth of the spout. In many cases it will look better and pour better if it is cut off horizontally and the lip is given a second turn to prevent dripping.

(24) Fit and fix the handle.

Fig. 213. The spout must always be level with the teapot top.

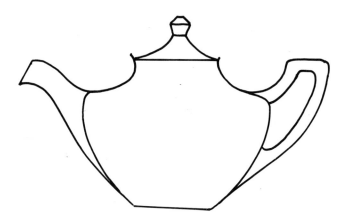

Fig. 212. A shape which is easier to cast than to throw.

Fig. 214. General balance must be maintained between spout and handle.

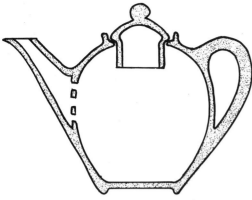

Fig. 215. Section through the fully designed teapot.

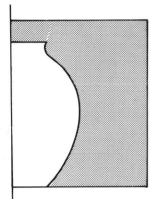

Fig. 216. Template of the profile.

Fig. 217. Stages in throwing a spout.

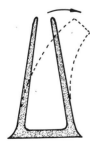

Fig. 218. Newly thrown spout bent over to improve pouring action.

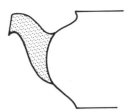

Fig. 219. A card template of the spout must be cut to fit the profile of the teapot.

Fig. 220. Each half of the spout is moulded on one of the two templates.

Fig. 221. Solid modelled spout with large and small cones added.

Fig. 222. Ledges between spout and cones must not be undercut.

Fig. 223. The two halves of a plaster mould (left and right), a cast spout (centre), and a finished teapot (top).

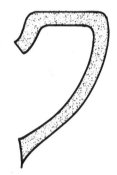

Fig. 224. A handle need not always be curved.

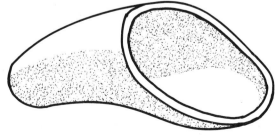

96   Fig. 225. Spout cut to fit the shape of the teapot.

Fig. 226. Perforations behind the spout. Note allowance for the slip area.

Fig. 227. Hole cutter.

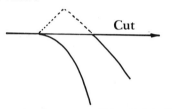

Cut

Fig. 228. A spout is often neater if levelled in line with the teapot top.

DECORATION

Traditional blue Wedgwood ware, with its finely modelled white relief decoration, is well-known and can be seen in most good china shops. Decorate each side of the teapot with a raised motif along these lines. The motif can be in the same clay, or clay of a different colour can be used. Take care not to merge the two colours when cleaning up; it is often better to wait until the decoration is drier, and tidy it up with a small scraper.

(1) Make some sketches for this motif, which can be abstract, pictorial, or geometric in character. It should be designed so that each raised portion links on to the next to form one composite unit.

(2) Model the motif on a flat slab of clay (see Assignment 14).

(3) Clean up the modelled motif, erect a clay wall round it, and pour in some plaster to make a cast.

When the plaster has set, remove the clay original and dry the plaster in a warm place.

(4) The modelled side of the cast must be absolutely flat. Rub it lightly, in a circular motion, on a sheet of fine glasspaper resting on a perfectly flat surface. Watch the effect of this carefully, and do not remove too much. Brush off any plaster dust.

(5) With the thumbs, press some clay over the mould, pushing it well down into the recesses. Using a slightly dampened palette knife, make the clay level with the flat plaster surface. Leave it for a little while to let the plaster absorb water from the clay, causing it to shrink slightly.

(6) Using a small dab of clay as a suction pad, lift the cast completely out of the mould. The relief portions of the design, but not the background, will have been moulded in clay. This thin relief, which is known as a sprig, must be handled delicately. It is advisable to scrap the first one or two pressings, since they will pick up odd bits of plaster dust left over from the levelling process.

(7) Coat the back of the sprig and the corresponding position on the teapot with a thin layer of slip, and lightly press one on the other. The sprig is sufficiently thin and pliable to take on the contour of the ground on which it is stuck. It is important to press the sprig down from the centre outwards, so that no air pockets form and the slip spreads evenly all the way round towards the outer edge.

(8) Lightly clean and sponge the edges.

(9) Biscuit-fire the completed teapot.

(10) Use any glaze, unless the sprigs are in a contrasting colour, in which case only transparent glaze should be used.

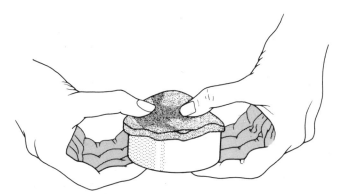

Fig. 230. *Filling a sprig mould with clay.*

Fig. 231. *Levelling the clay in a sprig mould with a palette knife.*

Fig. 229. *Initial modelling for a sprig mould.*

Fig. 232. *Removing a completed sprig with a dab of clay.*

97

Fig. 233. *Components of a teapot: thrown and formed spouts, and a handle (left and right), a sprig and a sprig mould (foreground), the basic pot (right), and the completed decorated teapot (top).*

Assignment 16 – off the Wheel

Hors d'oeuvre Set

NO BASIC POTTERY COURSE would be complete without providing some experience in double casting. In Assignments 8 and 12 the technique of making and using drain moulds was described. A mould of the outside of the object was made, deflocculated slip poured in and after a time poured out again, thus making a hollow casting. However this is clearly not an ideal method for objects required to have a specific, uniform thickness, since it depends on several variables such as the time the slip remains in the mould, and the porosity of the plaster which will become progressively less after each cast has been made.

To ensure casts of even thickness, a mould is made of both the inside and outside of the object, and the slip fills the space between them – this is known as double casting. An entry hole has to be made through which the slip can be poured; when making plates and dishes, this is ingeniously utilised as a small drain mould for casting the foot.

A set of dishes for serving hors d'oeuvre or salads can be considered in this context, since a number of identical containers will be required.

DESIGN

Decide how many dishes are required to make up the set. Think how they would best be arranged on the table – this will influence their shape and size. If you have the expertise, consider making a wooden tray to hold the finished dishes. This would be both attractive and space-saving. Decide on the most effective general size. Shape is an integral factor of both size and arrangement. The depth of the dishes, and the profile of the sides, are also important. Remember that sharp angles are not pleasant in clay, which is essentially a plastic medium.

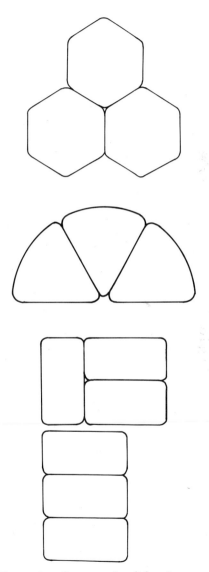

Fig. 234. Suggestions for arranging dish units.

WORK SEQUENCE AND DECORATION

(1) Cut two card templates, one of the plan of the dish and another of its profile or elevation. The elevation template can be cut in tin plate.

(2) Place the plan template on a flat board and build up a hump of clay on it, checking the sides against the template – the top must be flat. Smooth this hump into as good and true a finish as possible.

(3) Surround this with a casting-box, leaving a gap all round of about $1\frac{1}{4}$ in. (30 mm.). Seal all the corners of the box, mix some plaster, and fill the box to a depth of about 1 in. (24 mm.) above the clay hump. Allow the plaster to set thoroughly.

(4) Remove the clay. A plaster will remain, bearing the impression of the clay as a hollow. Lightly clean the edges of the hollow to check against any undercutting, and soap-size it. Also size the edges, in case of overflow.

(5) Again surround it with the casting-box, seal the joints with clay, and pour in enough plaster to bring the level up to about $1\frac{1}{4}$ in. (30 mm.) above the level of the first cast. Allow ample time for this to become really hard.

(6) Remove the box, plunge the plaster in a bowl of cold water, and separate the two portions. This now provides a plaster bearing the dish shape as a mound – in fact, it is a plaster replica of the original clay. The first pouring was only a means to an end and is no longer required; hence it is termed the waste mould.

(7) The plaster bearing the hump constitutes the inner portion of the required mould. Draw a pencil line $\frac{1}{4}$ in. (6 mm.) from the base of the hump on the flat plaster, and all the way round it.

(8) Roll out between slats a flat slab of clay $\frac{1}{4}$ in. (6 mm.) thick, and from it cut a shaped piece which will exactly fit over the plaster hump; the pencil mark will act as a guide so that the correct thickness is maintained all the way round. Problems of bending will arise at the corners, as a complicated development would normally be necessary to achieve the hump

shape. Compensate for this by cutting out a 'V' shape in the clay at the corners. If slightly too much clay is cut away, a little extra clay can be added to make up the thickness to the pencil line. Finish by carefully smoothing the surface of the clay.

(9) Decide on the size of foot needed. It will be the same shape as the dish, but, of course, much smaller. Make a card template of the size required.

(10) Roll out a flat piece of clay $1\frac{1}{4}$ in. (30 mm.) thick, and from it cut a piece the shape of the template. Taper it evenly on all sides.

(11) Fix this with a little slip to the top of the clay covering, with the sides tapering upwards. Make sure that the bottom edges are clean and sharp.

(12) Use the handle of a teaspoon to make four knatch holes in the corners of the plaster slab which carried the hump. This will assist correct registration.

(13) Soap-size the plaster, including the edges. Fix the casting-box in place round it, seal the edges, and pour plaster into the box to a level just below the top of the foot piece. This pour constitutes the second half of the mould.

(14) When the plaster is set, separate the two portions of the mould, remove the clay covering and the solid plug, and blunt the corners to make it easier to handle. If the two portions are now replaced, one on top of the other, it will be seen that there is a $\frac{1}{4}$ in. (6 mm.) space between them, which is the shape of the required dish, and a gap at the top which is the shape of the required foot.

(15) Allow enough time for the two halves of the mould to dry out. Then place them in apposition and slowly pour in some deflocculated slip, which will fill the cavity between the two parts, and the well. After about fifteen minutes the dish itself will have hardened, since it is thin and between two absorbent plaster surfaces. The slip in the well will still be fluid, except round the edges next to the plaster. This surplus slip is now drained off as a miniature drain mould, to leave a foot (far taller than is required).

(16) As soon as this foot has hardened, the two halves

of the mould can be separated and the cast dish taken off.

(17) Sponge the edges, and cut the tall foot down to the desired height. Variety is possible here: some designs may call for a fairly high foot, others a very shallow one, like those on side plates. The best way to do this is to prepare a block of wood of the correct height, and then trim the clay with a knife resting flat on the block. Soften the edges by sponging.

(18) As many dishes as required can be cast from the mould, and each will be of identical size and thickness. Since the foot is drained, slight variations may occur in its thickness, but this does not matter since the foot will rest on the table and not be visible.

(19) These dishes can be decorated in any way that appeals, but since together they form a composite unit it may be best if the decoration includes some unifying factor.

(20) Biscuit-fire the dishes, and glaze them. As an alternative to textural or applied decoration, consider glazing each dish in a different colour.

Fig. 237. The solid foot added.

Fig. 238. Stages in making a two-piece mould. In the centre is a dish straight from the mould before the foot is cleaned.

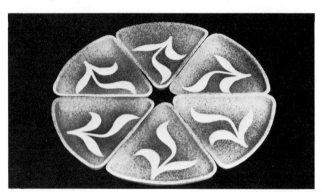

Fig. 239. Decorated hors d'oeuvre set, ready for glazing.

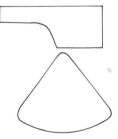

Fig. 235. Plan and elevation templates for the dish.

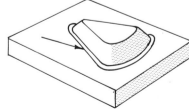

Fig. 236. The arrow shows the outside line of the covering clay.

Fig. 240. Levelling the foot of a cast dish, with the aid of a wood block and palette knife.

Assignment 17 –
on and off the Wheel
Composite Shapes

Fig. 241. Typical composite pot: components (left), and the completed pot (right).

SOME OF THE MOST visually interesting pots are a combination of thrown and hand-built work. The bulb pot in Assignment 11 is a simple example of this kind of pottery.

DESIGN

With this in mind, design a pot made up of two or more varied parts, each employing a different method, for instance a formed shape combined with a coiled one, a slab-built portion with a thrown top, or a thrown base with a hand-developed top. Experiment, too, with various combinations in shape: a rectangle with a cylinder, a round with an elliptical form, triangular shapes, or octagonal shapes with rounds and rectangles. Pay particular attention to the junction between the parts. Various problems can arise when working in three dimensions which are not apparent in a two-dimensional sketch. At the same time decide whether any added decoration is necessary in the form of a textured surface or some added relief or incising.

It is impossible to give a detailed work sequence or instructions for decoration, since every pot will be unique. The value of a project like this lies in the application of knowledge already gained to the solving of new problems, and in the opportunity to exercise your originality and creativity.

The pot in Fig. 241 will give some idea of the type of pot envisaged. It has a thrown neck luted on to a slab-built base. This particular piece highlights one or two practical aspects of procedure which will certainly apply to some designs.

It is necessary to plan the work systematically, and look ahead. It would be difficult, for example, to stamp the pattern relief in the side of the slab at any other stage than while the clay was still damp and before the base was assembled.

Note also that if the rectangular container was made complete with top and bottom, and then joined on to the turned neck, it would be impossible to cut the cavity between the two portions; the process of pressing on the neck and luting it exerts considerable pressure on the top, which would be liable to cave in. A recommended joining-up sequence in this case would be as follows: join a large side of the rectangle with a small side, and make one corner. Repeat with the remaining two sides for the opposite corner. Join both corners. Join the neck to the top. Hollow out the necessary portion. Lute the combined neck and top to the rectangular sides. Finally, join on the base. Each portion will normally require to be in the leather-hard state before assembly.

Dry the finished pot slowly, to avoid any cracking between parts. When fully dry, biscuit-fire and glaze as appropriate.

Assignment 17 – off the Wheel

Pew Group

IN ASSIGNMENT 6 CLAY figurines were made, which began as matchstick men drawings. When translated into the medium of clay, the lines and dots became rolls and balls of clay. The figures were then dressed with appropriate pieces of clothing. The same technique of matchstick drawings and rolls of clay can be used to make a clay animal. The animal will not, of course, need to be clothed; but the body can be textured with tiny clay rolls and dots to simulate hair, wool, or fur.

One of the problems encountered in making figurines was the provision of adequate support, especially for standing figures. There are various methods of overcoming the problem. One is to have the figurine sit down or lean against some appropriate prop. Alternatively, the figures can be joined to a wall of clay at the back, which is then modelled to create a suitable background.

Instead of a simple figurine, try now to design a small group of two or three people, and possibly a pet animal for additional interest. A school of Staffordshire potters created some very lovely little groups of this sort around 1730–1740, working in either salt-glazed stoneware or earthenware. Many of the groups were seated on a settle, which solved several design problems. The back of the traditional oak settle was solid and plain, so little reverse modelling was necessary, and the fact that the figures were seated solved the problem of support, for they could be modelled to the settle. These groups are often referred to in pottery books as pew groups. If possible, pay a visit to the Victoria and Albert Museum in London, or any other local museum where they are on display. The local public library should have books with illustrations of this kind of figure group.

DESIGN

The piece is to consist of two or more figurines, with an animal if appropriate. All the figures are to be well supported by a large background of clay, the back of which is to be left plain. The modelling is to be viewed from the front and sides. Fig. 242 shows a man and his wife lazing on a garden seat on a hot summer evening. The man is so tired that he dozes. As a result, the bored dog transfers its affections to the lady, who is still awake. Some other suggestions are two or three people sheltering from the rain in a porch or doorway – a cat shelters with them; a farmer's wife and her child feeding an orphan lamb in front of a kitchen fire; two clergymen poring over a reference book before a large bookcase; a bride and bridegroom in front of a church door; two guitar players, the background consisting of a large drum and other percussion instruments.

Fig. 242. Pew group, ready for biscuit-firing.

WORK SEQUENCE

(1) Make rough sketches of the intended composition. Visualise and sketch the linking prop and a method of making it into a convincing background. In certain cases this will require some ingenuity, since it must present a continuous backcloth, the back of which will be left plain. If, for instance, the figures are to be placed on a backless seat, the background must be extended upwards and filled in with appropriate details such as branches or flowers.

(2) Draw the proposed figurines as matchstick people.

(3) Roughly model the background. Make sure it is not too thick and solid. If it needs to be deep, hollow it out from the bottom. This will prevent it breaking during firing.

(4) Translate the matchstick figures into roll and ball clay figures. Remember that they must be in proportion with the size of the props already made. When figures are made, for instance, to sit on a seat, their legs should rest on the ground. Place the matchstick figures in the position they are to occupy in relation to the background prop, and leave them to harden a little. Do not fix them into position at this stage, as it is far easier to be able to pick them up to add clothing.

(5) When they are hard enough to handle without becoming mis-shapen, clothe them with shaped pieces cut from clay rolled out between $\frac{1}{8}$ in. (3 mm.) slats (see Assignment 6). Add any interesting extras to set the scene and the mood – a pipe, a dangling shoelace, a buttonhole flower, or an elbow patch.

(6) If an animal is to be included, treat this in the same way.

(7) Now place the figures and the animal on the prop or against it, painting generous pools of slip at the contact points, and modelling together where possible.

(8) Build up the background in as interesting a way as possible. If the background is a fluid shape – a shrub, for instance, or cushions – build this round the figures to give extra rigidity. All additions should be joined on with slip, and lightly luted wherever possible.

Do not trap hollow pockets of air at any point: examine the work and puncture with a needle any places which might contain air pockets; a modelled helmet on a policeman's head, for instance, can be ventilated by puncturing the top.

(9) Allow the composition to dry, and then biscuit-fire it.

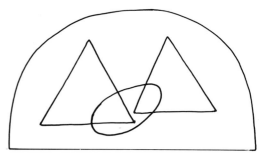

Fig. 243. Sketch showing the composition of the group.

DECORATION

(1) Decorate the group with a little under-glaze colour.

(2) When dry, coat it with transparent glaze.

(3) Alternatively, glaze in an opaque coloured glaze as a substitute for applied decoration.

Many of the historical groups of figures seen in museums are decorated with enamel colours on the fired glaze. Such enamels extend the possible colour range, but can only be successfully applied to stoneware or porcelain.

Assignment 18 – on the Wheel

Cider Bottle Shape

THE TRADITIONAL CIDER bottle is one of the more difficult shapes to throw, since the neck is sharply gathered-in from a full round shoulder.

DESIGN

The general form is a traditional one, but there is still some opportunity for variation. Decide on the size, and the proportion of height to width. Consider the shape beneath the round shoulders and experiment with a slow taper, a fuller taper, a continuous outward curve, a continous inward curve, or even a vertical profile.

Decide how high the neck should rise above the shoulders, and whether it ought to be straight, tapered, or curved. The top of the neck might be flared, shaped, straight, or turned over. Decide whether or not a lip is to be added. The shape, position, and size of the handle are important. Consider whether a pulled handle or a wire-cut handle are better in this instance. Wires can be made to cut a ribbed handle, which can be very attractive.

WORK SEQUENCE

(1) Prepare the clay well, and start work with a fair-sized ball. Centre, open the mass, and lift the wall to a cylinder of the required height, keeping the portion near the top thicker to allow for subsequent stretch when shaping the bulbous shoulder. Spin the wheel slightly faster than usual to centre this large piece of clay.

(2) Shape the body of the bottle. Bend the fingers of the left hand, and tuck the finger tips well up under the clay to shape the full shoulder. Do not let the left hand

Fig. 244. Cider bottle shapes.

Fig. 245. Wire for pulling a ribbed handle.

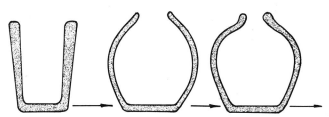

Fig. 246. Stages in throwing a cider bottle shape.

or wrist lean on the top of the clay, which should be kept as narrow as possible to save excessive gathering-in later.

(3) Gather-in the neck. On a bottle of this size place the thumb and first finger of each hand round the clay at the point where the neck is to begin, as though strangling it. Give a little pinch with both hands, and then move them vertically to the top of the clay without further inward pressure. Repeat this process as often as necessary until the neck is restricted to a diameter of roughly $2\frac{1}{2}$ in. (60 mm.). Now move the hands to the six-point contact position. Remember that gathering thickens the clay wall, and it must therefore be alter-

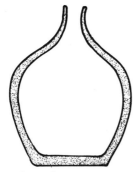

Fig. 247. Thinning the neck.

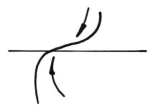

Fig. 248. Finger pressure when shaping the shoulder.

nated with periodic lifting from the base of the neck to the top. This is the tricky part of the exercise. If gathered-in too gradually, the result will be an ordinary bottle like the one in Assignment 9. If gathered too suddenly, the top will turn in on itself and collapse within the body. Try to gather-in on a line a little above the horizontal.

(4) Shape the neck itself, and give it a good finish at the top. A turned-over top can be very effective, and provides extremely good practice in handling clay; it is made as follows.

(5) Thin the top as much as possible, and make sure that it is absolutely level by trimming with the needle.

(6) Rest the index finger of the left hand against the outside of the neck about $\frac{1}{2}$ in. (12 mm.) from the top edge. Roll the top over this finger (using the index finger of the right hand) until it forms a hook shape.

(7) Trap the turned-over clay between the first finger and thumb of the left hand, and complete the turn-down against the side of the neck. Run the first finger of the right hand in the middle of the turned-down portion, to create an interesting concave collar.

(8) Pull the lip, if one is required.

(9) As the cider bottle has a narrow neck, it must be turned in a ring (see Assignment 9).

(10) Make the handle and, when sufficiently dry, fix it to the bottle.

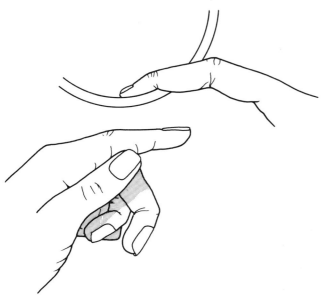

Fig. 249. First stage in turning a rim.

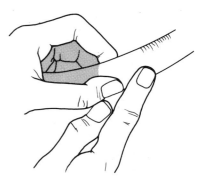

Fig. 250. Second stage in turning a rim.

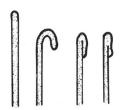

Fig. 251. Sections showing the stages in turning over a rim.

DECORATION

Design a wide border repeat for the cider bottle. It will be painted in the reverse method – in other words the background is to be painted, and the pattern itself left plain. This gives a similar effect to sgraffito decoration, except that the whole surface remains perfectly smooth and flat. Think in terms of large areas, as narrow lines are not very effective in this style of decoration. The pattern is to be further highlighted by leaving it unglazed, as hard biscuit.

(1) When the bottle has completely dried out, prepare about ¼ lb. (113 g.) of opaque glaze. The glaze should be dark for a bottle made in a light clay, and light in colour if the bottle is in red clay. Sieve the glaze with as little added water as possible, to keep it thick. At the same time, dissolve 1½ level teaspoons of powdered gelatine in 10 fl. oz. (0.3 litres) of cold water. Put the powder in a jar, add the water, stand the jar in a pan of hot water over a moderate heat, and stir until all the gelatine has dissolved. Add this solution to the glaze, and keep the mixture hot by standing the container in hot water, like a glue pot.

(2) Pour a little of the mixture into the cider bottle, swill the inside to glaze it, and pour out the surplus. Pick up the bottle carefully, and paint glaze on the base.

(3) Divide the circumference of the bottle into equal sections, and draw in the outline of the pattern with a pencil.

(4) Paint in the background areas of the pattern with the gelatinised glaze, using a soft mop brush. Use the glaze generously. The glaze cools as it comes into con-

Fig. 252. Two large bottles, one decorated with gelatinised glaze.

tact with the pot, and the gelatine sets it on the clay. The brush will become stiff as the gelatine sets in it, and it will need to be rinsed periodically in hot water to keep it supple. Remember that the pot is not yet biscuited, and therefore very brittle.

(5) When the background has been painted, glaze any remaining areas of the bottle with the same mixture. A thicker layer may be built up if desired, by adding a second layer on top of the first.

(6) After painting, handle the pot as little as possible to prevent the glaze layer smudging or flaking. It will be biscuited and glazed in one operation. This technique is more applicable to stoneware, which is vitreous when mature, but it can be used on earthenware provided the inside is glazed thoroughly.

107

Assignment 18 –
off the Wheel

Personal Ornaments

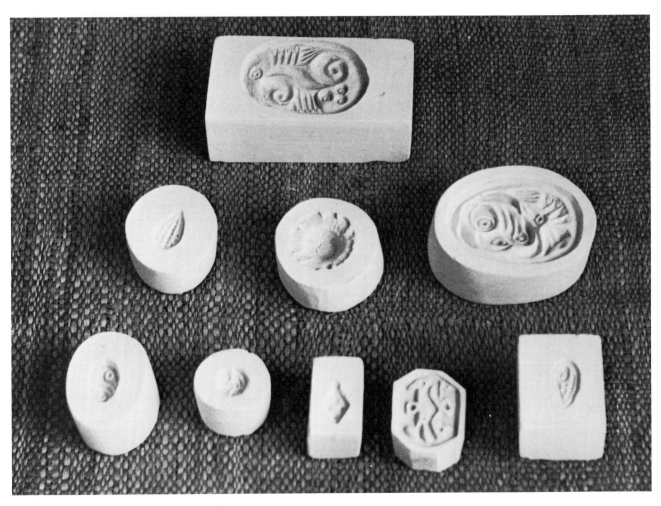

Fig. 253. Assorted plaster moulds for making personal ornaments.

THROUGHOUT HISTORY CLAY, both glazed and unglazed, has been used as a material for making personal ornaments. Examples can be found in most local museums. The British Museum in London has some fine examples of the skilled way in which the craftsmen of Ancient Egypt used the medium to make exquisite pectorals and beads. They worked with both clay, glazed in lovely blues, yellows, and greens, and a substance known as Egyptian paste, which can best be described as a type of solid modelling glaze.

Attractive pendants can be made on the lines of the wall hanging made in Assignment 14; pierce a hole at the top, through which to thread a piece of leather lacing. Small sprig moulds, as used for the teapot in Assignment 16, can be used to cast decorative tops for cuff-links; they can subsequently be fixed to cuff-link findings with an epoxy resin glue. Brooches and rings can also be made in this way. An ornamental piece for drop ear-rings can be made by modelling together, back to back, two pressings from a suitably-shaped mould.

Personal ornaments must inevitably include beads, and much ingenuity can be displayed in making them.

DESIGN

Think about general size, and decide whether or not there should be any gradation between the beads at the centre and those at the ends of the string. Consider whether all the beads on one necklace should be the same basic shape, or whether alternating forms would be attractive. It might be an idea to have a distinct feature bead at the centre, different from all the other beads.

Decide if the beads are to be glazed, and, if so, in what colour or colours. Give some thought to the diameter of the hole through which the thread will be passed. Remember that it will shrink when the beads are fired, and that if it is too small, glaze runs could block it altogether.

A number of techniques can be used, but there is a useful type of plaster mould, not previously mentioned, which can be used to produce beads, or a number of identical handles for cups, jugs, or mugs. Instructions are given below for making 'hip' shape beads by this method, which is known as press moulding.

WORK SEQUENCE

(1) Model in clay one bead of exact size and shape, but do not pierce it.
(2) When complete, bury it up to the half-way line in the centre of a clay block.
(3) Surround the block with a casting-box, seal it, and pour in sufficient plaster to make one half of the mould.
(4) When the plaster is set, remove the casting-box and the clay block.
(5) Cut knatch holes at the four corners of the plaster for registering, and soap-size the plaster surface.
(6) Put it back in the casting-box, and pour the second half of the mould.
(7) When the plaster is set, soak it in water and separate the two plaster halves.
(8) In each half cut away a channel round the bead shape with a hard modelling tool. The channels should be cut so that they leave a plaster cutting edge round the bead shape.
(9) Model a piece of fairly soft clay to the required shape, and place it in one half of the mould.
(10) Place the opposite half over it in the correct position (located by the knatch holes), and press the two parts hard together. Surplus clay is extruded into the surrounding channel, and finally cut off by the sharp plaster edge. This surplus clay can be removed on opening the mould.
(11) The bead will now require piercing. It may be found easier to cut a small semi-circular groove in a corresponding position at the centre of each half of the mould. One half of the mould can then be filled roughly with clay, and a knitting needle or similar object pressed into it so that its ends rest in the central grooves. The opposite half is roughly filled in a similar fashion, the clay surface in each half given a thin brush-coating of slip, and the two halves pressed together as before. On

completion, the needle can be withdrawn.

A mould of this type is very suitable for producing a number of small objects quickly, since little drying time is required between pressings.

Here is another idea to develop. Experiment with pieces of paper cut to various shapes and lengths, and roll them round a knitting needle. Roll out a very thin piece of clay, cut it to the same shape as the paper, and roll it round the needle. Fix the end with a spot of slip, and lightly model it.

Be adventurous – coil tiny rolls of clay; add tiny pieces of contrasting clay as a decoration on plain beads; model small blocks of clay and carve them when they are leather-hard – the possibilities are endless.

The pectoral in Fig. 260 was inspired by a visit to the Egyptology section of the British Museum. It looks very complicated, but in fact no part of it is difficult to make; it is only the assembly that requires patience and application.

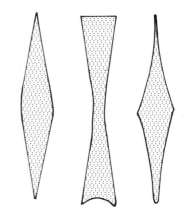

Fig. 256. *Trial shapes for rolling beads.*

Fig. 254. *'Hip'-shaped bead.*

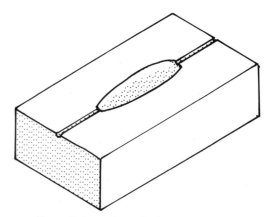

Fig. 257. *Central channel cut for knitting needle.*

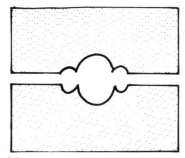

Fig. 255. *Section through the press mould.*

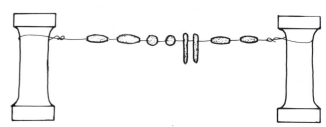

Fig. 258. *Beads strung on nichrome wire for glaze-firing.*

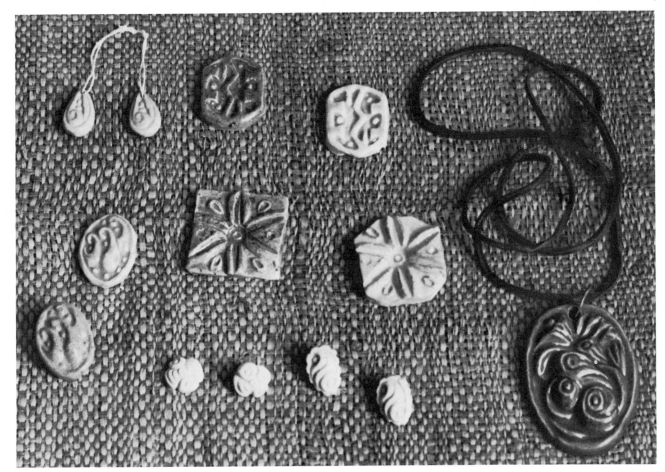

Fig. 259. Ceramic jewellery.

DECORATION

The ornaments can be decorated using any of the techniques previously described. If they are to be glazed, always check that the holes are clear of glaze before firing. It is best to paint glaze on to beads, and not bring it too near the holes.

A note on firing

Glazed pendants and larger pieces of jewellery can be fired on a three-point stilt. A problem arises where glazed beads and small ear-rings are concerned. Use nichrome wire to thread them on – the wire is hung like a clothes-line between two fireclay pillars in the kiln. Keep the wire fairly taut, or some of the beads may slip down and link themselves up. The wire may be used for many firings.

Clay

CLAY HAS ITS ORIGIN in feldspathic rock which has been decomposed by aeons of weathering and the action of water, carbonated by humus in the soil. During the process, any soluble salts of soda, potash or lime are dissolved out, and the result is clay, a mineral made up of the remaining aluminium, silica and water.

In chemical terms, this is what happens to orthoclase (potash feldspar):

$$6H_2O + CO_2 + 2KAlSi_3O_8 \longrightarrow$$

$$\text{CARBONATED WATER} + \text{ORTHOCLASE} \longrightarrow$$

$$Al_2Si_2O_5(OH)_4 + 4SiO_24H_2O + K_2CO_3$$

CLAY + SILICIC ACID + POTASSIUM CARBONATE

which dissolves out

A similar action takes place in the case of the soda and lime feldspars. In some tropical climates the silica also was removed, and the resultant mineral, bauxite, is the ore from which aluminium is extracted.

To know the origin of clays is a great help in understanding why some clays, notably china clay (kaolin), found in certain areas such as St. Austell in Cornwall, have to be obtained the hard way. This involves washing the deposit with powerful hoses, and recovering the clay from the resultant suspension. Some clays, on the other hand, can be dug with a spade, possibly even in your own back garden.

Certain clays, like the china clay mentioned, remain in the exact place in which they were formed, and are known as residual clays. In other instances, clays were formed in the catchment areas of streams and rivers. As a result, they have been gradually eroded by the scouring action of the fast tumbling waters, and carried along in suspension, sometimes for long distances. As the streams reached lower levels, they naturally slowed down, and consequently tended to drop the suspended clay particles which had become finely ground by the action of the water. This is the beginning of the clay bed from which finely-particled clay can be dug. Clays which have been re-deposited away from the locality of their formation are known as sedimentary clays.

It is an interesting point that china clay is obtained by the action of an artificial water source, thus making a parallel with the action of nature in producing sedimentary clays.

These two types of clays possess very different characteristics.

Residual	Sedimentary
Non-plastic	Very plastic
Very refractory	Not very refractory
Very strong	—
Fairly coarse	Finely particled

Fig. 260. A finished pectoral.

On consideration of these qualities it is clear that, for most articles, the potter would find it desirable to incorporate some of the features of each type of clay. In some cases plasticity will be more of an asset than, say, the ability to withstand a high temperature. Plant breeders developing new strains or varieties cross-pollinate known species, each having one desirable feature, and hope in this way to combine in one plant the optimum features of a number of others. In a similar way, clays are blended in varying proportions to make the end product fit its intended purpose.

In a throwing clay, for instance, plasticity is vitally important; on the other hand insulators for high voltage equipment demand high refractive qualities. It is desirable, on occasions, that a clay product should be dense and vitreous, and behave in the fire rather like a glaze. Clays for throwing become very wet, and therefore need to be very porous to avoid warping during the drying stage. All these considerations must be taken into account when compounding mixtures of clay.

These clay blends are commonly known as bodies. The common earthenware bodies obtainable from suppliers contain a good percentage of sedimentary ball clay to make them very plastic, some china clay to make them strong, and some flint and Cornish stone to make them porous and sufficiently refractory to withstand a firing temperature of about 1100°C. The red body contains a high percentage of naturally occurring iron.

There are three main types of ware. Earthenware is the name given to pottery which is still porous when fired, and so needs a glaze to render it fully waterproof. A flower-pot is an earthenware article.

With less sedimentary clay, more flint and more china clay, a body can be made which will fire at about 1230°C.; when fired, it is extremely hard and completely vitreous. Although a glaze is usually added for aesthetic reasons, the fired product is fully waterproof. This is stoneware.

The third group of ware is known as porcelain, which, when fired at a temperature between 1300°C. and 1500°C., becomes translucent. The body contains a large proportion of refractory materials and fluxes.

The action of firing renders clay irreversibly hard. The actual changes are very complex, but may be briefly summarised like this.
(1) Physical water is lost.
(2) Chemically combined water is lost, and matter becomes coagulated. Shrinkage takes place.
(3) Above 1000°C. the alumina and silica in the clay combine to form mullite ($Al_2O_3.SiO_2$).
(4) In porcelain, partial fusion takes place.
(5) If subjected to higher temperatures (1700°C.—1800°C.), the clay will fuse to a viscous liquid.

Temperature of fusion will vary considerably between one clay or one body and another, and in some cases can be as low as the 1200°C.—1300°C. range.

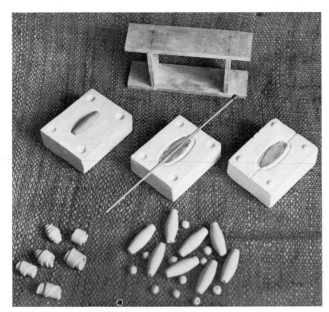

Fig. 261. Bead mould (centre), beads made in it (bottom right), and rolled beads (bottom left).

Firing

THE PIECES IN THESE assignments can be fired in an electric kiln suitable for firing earthenware, in which work to be fired can be directly packed. Each piece is twice fired, once to mature the clay, and once to melt the glaze. Earthenware is fired to maturity as biscuit, and then glazed at a lower temperature. This is the reverse of high temperature wares, such as stoneware, where the biscuit is fired to the relatively low temperature of 850°C. and given a high fire after the glaze has been applied; glaze and body mature at the same time.

When packing a biscuit kiln, always aim to accommodate as much as possible. However, the temptation to over-pack must be avoided, especially round the edges of the kiln, where enough space must be left to allow adequate heat circulation. Standard kiln furniture includes a number of heat-porous fireclay shelves which are best supported on castellated props so that the height can be varied. Part shelves too are invaluable, and make it possible to include one or two very tall pots together with others of more normal height (a single tall pot will waste kiln space, as a whole shelf may have to be removed to accommodate it). Rest each shelf on three rather than four prop pillars, as this will eliminate rocking; it is also important to place prop pillars directly above each other on consecutive shelves.

Before packing a kiln, grade all the pots for height, to assist efficient packing. Pieces can touch one another without damage in the biscuit kiln, so no space need be left between them. Certain economy measures assist space saving.

(1) Bowls, cups, mugs etc. with the same size mouths can be inverted, one on the other, to rest rim-to-rim. However, one bowl with a slightly smaller mouth should never be upturned over another, as it might jam when the clay shrinks, and also distort the sides of the larger bowl.

114

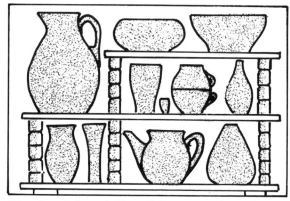

Fig. 262. A short shelf can help accommodate a large pot.

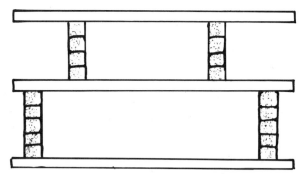

Fig. 263. Shelf supports must never be arranged like this, but directly on top of each other.

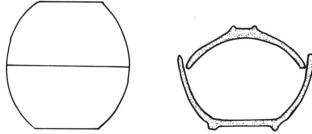

Fig. 264 (left). Bowls may be inverted rim to rim.

Fig. 265 (right). One pot must not be stacked within the sides of another.

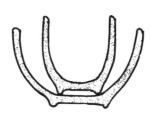

Fig. 266 (left). Lids can be inverted to save height.

Fig. 267 (right). One pot may be fired within another, provided the feet are immediately above one another.

(2) Smaller articles can be fired inside larger ones, provided one stands above the foot of the other.
(3) When packing covered pots, the lid can be turned inside out, to save height.
(4) Small items, such as mosaic pieces, can be fired on the kiln shelf between other pots and pieces of modelling.

Pieces must be checked before packing, to make sure that they are thoroughly dry. Red and white earthenware bodies usually mature at a different temperature, so if possible have one firing for each type of body. Mixed firing often means satisfactory red ware, and white ware which crazes when glazed.

The kiln temperature can be measured with a built-in pyrometer, or by temperature cones incorporated in the packing. The pyrometer measures temperature, and the cones measure heat work. Seger cones are widely used, but suppliers now also retail the American Orton cones which many potters consider superior. Cones are made so that they bend or squat (the term normally used) at a specified temperature. Seger and Orton cones do not always carry the same numbers for the same squatting temperatures. A comparative table is given, for easy reference when deciding which cone to use.

Orton cone	Seger cone	Squatting temp. °C.
022	022	600
021	022A	614
020	021	635
019	019	683
018	018	717
017	016	747
016	015	792
015	014	804
014	013	838
013	012	852
012	011	884
011	010	894
010		894
09	09	923
08	08A	955
07	06	984
06	05	999
05	03A	1046
04	02	1060
03	1	1101
02	2	1120
01	3	1137
1	3A	1154
2	4	1162
3	4A	1168
4	5A	1186
5	6	1196
6	7	1222
7	7A	1240
8	8A	1263
9	9	1280
10	10	1305

Reproduced by courtesy of the Edward Orton Jr. Ceramic Foundation, Columbus, Ohio.

Pyrometric cones are used in threes. The middle one is chosen to bend at the required temperature, the first just below it, and the last just above it. The cone

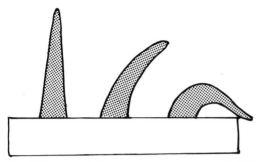

Fig. 268. Silhouette of Seger cones after a successful firing.

registering the lowest temperature bends early to give warning that the kiln temperature is approaching the maximum required, and that more frequent inspection is called for. Firing should continue until the cone which indicates the required temperature just begins to bend. The last cone, representing a higher temperature, should still appear straight if the kiln is not over-fired. Cones are supported on specially made sockets, and should be packed into the kiln so that they can easily be observed from the spy-hole on the kiln door. Seger cones always bend away from the ⋈ sign, Orton cones towards the ⚓ sign. Failure to remember this can often ruin a pot placed near the cones in a glaze kiln.

Biscuit kilns should be fired very slowly in the initial stages. Although the pots are considered dry, extra moisture will appear at the kiln vent, the bung of which must be left out to allow the water vapour to escape. If a cold object is held over the vent it will steam up. Even when all the physical moisture has been driven off by the heat, chemically combined water still remains in the clay, and this also must find an exit. Water is being lost up to well above 600°C., and firing must proceed very slowly.

Above 750°C. the firing can be speeded up to maximum rate, and the vent bung re-inserted. If a regulator is fitted into the kiln circuit, this should read not more than 25 at first, and be maintained in that position for a minimum of four hours. Gradual advancement is then

necessary over the next two or three hours to a setting of 75, when it is safe to apply full heat. A very satisfactory arrangement is to commence firing overnight, leaving the regulator at the 25 reading. The firing can then be advanced next morning. Cooling should be natural, and opening of the kiln should not be hurried.

Extra care is necessary when packing a glaze kiln, since any pots which touch will emerge at the end of the fire as 'Siamese twins'. To render it absolutely waterproof, earthenware should be well glazed all over, and it is better to fire the pots on refractory supports rather than clean off much of the glaze from the lower portion of the pot, as is customary when firing stoneware.

Fig. 269. Small electric kiln packed for a glaze-fire. Note that a pot in the bottom right-hand corner has tilted off its stilt. This can easily happen, so the contents of the kiln should always be checked before firing.

The usual support is the porcelain stilt, which is available in sizes 01—07, from small to large. The supports have three upward points and three downward points, and are intended to support the pot on the turned foot. Glaze sometimes runs off the foot of a pot and forms a small pool on the kiln shelf. Each shelf should be painted with a flint wash (this will not vitrify during firing); it will then be easy to clean off these small spills after each firing. Modelled pieces can be cleaned at the base, and fired directly on the kiln shelf – they do not need to be completely watertight.

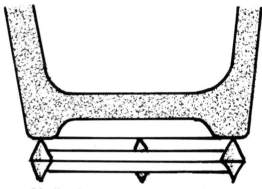

Fig. 270. Ideally, the points of a stilt should rest on the turned foot of the pot.

A problem arises when packing lids, since they often fall between two stilt sizes. Wash the glaze off the bottom edge and for a few millimetres up the side; this portion will normally sit within the pot flange when in use, and will not therefore be visible.

Pots must be handled very carefully, as glaze can easily be removed at touch points, and in majolica ware the pattern can be damaged. Any bald patches left by finger marks must be touched up with more glaze. One more word of warning: when packing pots covered with glazes of varying colour, beware of carrying glaze on your fingers from one pot to another. It is infuriating to see a beautifully glazed pot marred by finger prints of another colour.

The glaze kiln can be fired rather more rapidly, since drying out is limited only to the water in the glaze – there is none in the clay itself by this time. A preliminary drying period of two or three hours at the 25 setting is sufficient, after which firing can progress rapidly to the maximum setting. The vent bung should be left out during the fire to allow carbon dioxide and other gases to escape. If trapped in the kiln, they can cause blistering of the glaze. At the end of the firing the bung should be replaced so that the kiln cools evenly. On no account must the kiln be opened before the ware is cold; a sudden chilling is one cause of crazing even in a glaze which otherwise fits the body.

When unpacking the kiln, the stilts can be tapped from the feet with a convenient instrument such as a turning tool. Vicious, razor-sharp slivers of stilt points often remain embedded in the glaze, and it is well worth the extra time to remove these as soon as the ware is taken from the kiln.

Finally, note that the kiln atmosphere in an electric kiln is an oxidising one. Reduction, which means robbing certain oxides in the glaze of part of their oxygen, is only possible in gas, wood, coke, or oil kilns, where the atmosphere can be rendered smoky and oxygen-hungry. This is a stoneware and not an earthenware technique, and has therefore not been dealt with in this book.

Glaze

GLAZING IS A VERY wide and complex subject, and this is intended to be only a general introduction.

Many pottery students use standard glazes compounded and tested by pottery suppliers, but it is still important that the nature of the material should be understood, and that some experience should be gained in compounding glazes from raw materials. Pottery is a craft that can rise to an art form, but ceramics is a definite science based on chemistry.

Glazes may be classified in a variety of ways. A simple distinction would be that some are transparent and shiny and allow decoration beneath to show through; others are opaque and shiny and blot out the colour of the clay upon which they are applied; while yet others are opaque and non-shiny, and are referred to as matt glazes.

They could be classified on the basis of melting temperatures; low temperature, earthenware, or soft glazes melting at a temperature between 900° and 1100°C.; stoneware glazes maturing within the range 1200°C.–1300°C.; and true high temperature porcelain glazes maturing within the range 1300°C.–1500°C.

A more useful method of classification, however, is based on the chemical composition of the glaze. To appreciate such a classification, an elementary knowledge is needed of the nature of glaze itself. When an acid reacts with a base, a salt is formed, and since glaze ingredients include both acidic and basic oxides it is tempting to assume that the fired glaze is the product of a similar reaction. This is, however, not entirely true, since proportions in a glaze formula are variable within limits, and this could never be the case if the product were a single pure chemical compound; the final glaze, too, would have a crystalline rather than a glassy texture. Glaze can be more accurately considered as a solution of a salt in one or more bases.

From a completely different viewpoint, the bases may be regarded as fluxing agents. The term is commonly used in connection with metal soldering, when certain substances known as fluxes are used to keep the metal chemically clean, and allow the solder to flow freely round the joint. The action of flowing is implied here also. Silica, one of the chief constituents of glaze, melts at a temperature higher than that attainable in the normal pottery kiln, and the bases must be added to cause the silica to melt or flow within a convenient temperature range.

Various oxides can be used as fluxes; some, notably lead oxide, bring the melting point down as low as 900°C. It is therefore useful to describe glazes by reference to their bases or fluxes. On this basis, the following terms are in common use:

Lead glaze
Leadless glaze
Alkaline glaze
Lead and soda glaze, etc.

If the two components – silica and a base – are ground together, made into a glaze, and applied to a pot, the mixture will melt satisfactorily to form a glaze but will probably run off the sides and form a neat pool of glaze at the bottom of the pot. Clearly, a glaze mixture needs a third constituent to inhibit its flowing property sufficiently for the molten glaze to remain *in situ* on the pot. The ingredient added is normally alumina (aluminium oxide), which is present in most clays. It is often referred to as an amphoteric, since it can act as either an acid or a base.

The three necessary parts of a glaze are therefore:
(1) Silica
(2) A basic flux or combination of fluxes
(3) Alumina.

Before leaving the question of classification, the distinction between a raw glaze and a fritted glaze should be noted. The word 'frit' is quite often seen in suppliers' catalogues; a frit is produced by fusing together certain dry parts of a glaze to form a glass, and then re-grinding the product to a powder which is incorporated in the final glaze. Glaze is applied as a suspension in water, so its ingredients must be insoluble. However, some desirable glaze materials, such as soda or boric acid, are soluble in water; but if these soluble ingredients are fritted with part of the silica, the powder produced is insoluble and the problem is solved. Lead oxide is a very poisonous substance which, if used, presents a health hazard. However, if the lead is fritted with the silica, it is made relatively safe to use. Lead frits are marketed as lead monosilicate, lead bisilicate, and lead sesquisilicate.

GLAZE BUILDING

If the following list of fluxes is studied:

Lead oxide	PbO
Sodium oxide	Na_2O
Potassium oxide	K_2O
Magnesium oxide	MgO
Zinc oxide	ZnO
Barium oxide	BaO
Calcium oxide	CaO

it will be observed that the formula of each contains one atom of oxygen. The acid silica, SiO_2, contains two atoms of oxygen, and the amphoteric alumina, Al_2O_3, three atoms of oxygen. This led the chemist Seger, when investigating the basic laws governing the building of glazes, to describe the fluxing oxides as the RO group – R standing for the metal, the silica as the RO_2 ingredient, and the amphoteric as the R_2O_3 ingredient. He also determined that there were certain proportional limits within which these three components could be successfully combined to form a glaze. Seger's findings form the basis of modern glaze building. All the fluxes introduced are reduced to a unit of 1, and on the Seger basis the silica content must be 2+, the upper limit being variable for glazes designed for firing at different temperatures. The proportion of amphoteric must be kept at less than 1; it is normally about 0.1—0.15 that of the silica.

This method of expressing a glaze formula shows the molecular proportions in which the ingredients go into solution. It is known as the Seger Formula, or the Molecular Glaze Formula, and can be stated as:

$$RO \qquad R_2O_3 \qquad RO_2$$

where RO is 1, R_2O_3 is less than 1, and RO_2 is twice 1, plus.

A specific Molecular Glaze Formula for an earthenware glaze might read like this:

RO		R_2O_3	RO_2
PbO	0.75	Al_2O_3 0.3	SiO_2 2.6
K_2O	0.1		
Na_2O	0.15		
Total	1		

When using the Seger Formula to compound a sample of glaze, raw materials must be selected to supply the required ingredients, and they must be in the correct proportion to satisfy the formula.

For the glaze above, the fluxing agent PbO could be supplied as litharge (PbO), as lead carbonate ($PbCO_3$), or red lead (Pb_3O_4). It has already been noted, when discussing frits, that these forms of lead are dangerous, so it would be sensible to introduce the required amount of PbO in the form of the frit lead monosilicate. The K_2O can be introduced as potash feldspar, and the soda as soda feldspar, both of which are insoluble in water; the alumina can be china clay and the silica flint.

Remember that the formula supplies proportions in the form of molecular parts, so to work out parts by weight for the glaze recipe a table will be needed, which either quotes the molecular weight of the substance to be used, or gives the atomic weights of the individual elements, from which the molecular weights can then be calculated.

The composition of the frit lead monosilicate can be represented as $PbO.SiO_2$, and its molecular weight is 283. To supply the 0.75 molecular parts of PbO called for by the Seger Formula, 0.75×283 parts by weight of the frit will be required. To obtain the required amount of potash, 0.1 molecular parts of potash feldspar must be added. The composition of this mineral is represented as $K_2O.Al_2O_3.6SiO_2$ (with a molecular weight of 556); $0.1 \times 556 = 55.6$, so 55.6 parts by weight will therefore be necessary in the recipe. This quantity of potash feldspar also adds 0.1 molecular parts of alumina (Al_2O_3) and $6 \times 0.1 = 0.6$ parts of silica.

Similarly, when soda feldspar $Na_2O.Al_2O_3.6SiO_2$ (with a molecular weight of 524) is used to supply the Na_2O, $0.15 \times 524 = 78.6$ parts by weight will be necessary; at the same time another $0.15 \times 6 = 0.9$ parts of silica will have been supplied to the glaze.

When deciding on the final amount of china clay needed to make up the complement of alumina, the quantity already supplied by the two feldspars (0.25 molecular parts) must be taken into account, so that only 0.3 minus $0.25 = 0.05$ molecular parts will be needed by the direct addition of china clay. China clay itself can be considered as being made up of alumina, silica, and water, with a molecular weight of 258, and is represented as $Al_2O_3.2SiO_2.2H_2O$, so that $0.05 \times 258 = 12.9$ parts by weight must be added to the recipe. However, the complex nature of china clay means that by adding 0.05 parts of alumina, 0.1 molecular parts of silica are added as well. The two molecular parts of water are lost as steam during firing.

To complete the recipe, consideration must be given to the amount of flint required, since the following parts will already have been supplied to the glaze:

0.75 parts from the lead monosilicate
0.6 parts from the potash feldspar
0.9 parts from the soda feldspar
0.1 parts from the china clay

totalling 2.35 molecular parts altogether out of the 2.6 parts called for. Therefore only 0.25 molecular parts of flint, which is pure silica, will need to be added. Flint has a molecular weight of 60, so that the final recipe must include $0.25 \times 60 = 15$ parts by weight.

The recipe will therefore read as follows:

Lead monosilicate	212.25
Potash feldspar	55.60
Soda feldspar	78.60
China clay	12.90
Flint	15.00

It could also be expressed as a percentage recipe, by dividing each quantity by the total, and multiplying by 100:

Lead monosilicate	56.70
Potash feldspar	14.85
Soda feldspar	21.00
China clay	3.45
Flint	4.00
	100.00

COLOUR IN GLAZES

Colour is produced by adding metallic oxides to the basic glazes, but the resultant colour will vary with the type of glaze to which the oxide is added. The details in the table opposite apply to earthenware glazes only.

It must be emphasised that colour can vary to a great extent, depending on the percentages of colouring agent used, the colour of the clay beneath the glaze, firing schedules, and the position of the piece in the kiln in relation to other glazed pieces. A pot with a chrome glaze, for instance, can become pink if placed in the kiln next to another containing tin (stannic) oxide.

The colouring oxides can be mixed, and it is interesting to experiment and tabulate the results. Direct colours can sometimes be a little glaring. Iron chromate is a very useful additive; it is a greying agent and produces a much quieter effect. It is also possible to stain glazes by adding under-glaze colours and the specially compounded stains sold by pottery suppliers.

Opaque glazes can be made from any transparent

glaze by adding ten per cent of stannic oxide. This is the majolica glaze used in Assignment 6. Alternatively, ten to fifteen per cent of zirconium oxide or 'zircon' (zirconium silicate) may be added to the transparent glaze.

Matt glaze can be produced in a number of ways, some of which require manipulation of the basic molecular formula or the temperature of firing, but the addition of twenty per cent of whiting to a transparent glaze is an easy, straightforward method of making it matt.

Oxide	%	Lead glaze	Alkaline glaze
CuO (copper)	1—6	green	green— turquoise
CoO (cobalt)	0.5—3	blue	vivid blue
Fe_2O_3 (iron)	5—10	golden browns— dark browns	straw— tans— dark browns
MnO_2 (manganese)	5—10	purple— brown	plum

MAKING UP GLAZE FROM A RECIPE

To make up a glaze from a recipe, weigh out the ingredients and grind them well together in a large mortar. Colouring agents need to be added in small quantities, and they should be weighed out on a chemical balance. For this reason it is often best to keep to metric measurements. Grinding is especially important when colouring oxides are incorporated. Cobalt oxide, for example, if not properly ground, can impart a blue speckle to the glaze. There will of course be times when this is a desirable feature.

When the ingredients have been well ground in the dry state, add a little water and allow it to soak into the powdery mass, then add a little more water to make it into a wet slurry. Re-grind, continuing to add small quantities of water from time to time until the glaze is mobile. Now sieve the mixture through a 120's lawn into a plastic or enamelled storage bucket, and cover it. The ingredients will tend to settle if the glaze is not used immediately, but provided it is not allowed to dry out, it can be stirred again without the need for re-sieving.

Glazes purchased ready-made from the suppliers, in powder form, still require sieving before use.

Generally speaking, transparent glazes should be used thinly, and opaque and matt glazes much more thickly. The following proportions of water to glaze should prove adequate, but it is always advisable to first glaze a small test piece. Any necessary adjustment can then be made to the glaze, either by adding more water, or by allowing the glaze to settle so that excess water can be removed.

Transparent glaze		Opaque glaze	
glaze	water	glaze	water
18 oz.	20 fl. oz. (1 pint)	26 oz.	20 fl. oz. (1 pint)
(3.2 kg.)	(1 litre)	(4.6 kg.)	(1 litre)

Since so many glazes look alike in the liquid state, always remember to label each batch of glaze clearly as soon as it is prepared.

APPLYING GLAZE

The aim is to cover the pot with an even layer of glaze. Dipping, spraying, pouring, and painting are all methods in common use, and the choice depends on the quantity of glaze prepared, the equipment available, the size and form of the pot, and the decoration which is worked on the pot.

If a bucketful of glaze is available, and the pot will fit conveniently inside, dipping is both rapid and effective. It is always the best method when glazing shallow dishes, plates, and tiles. Hold the biscuited piece in as few fingers as possible, swirl it and lift it out. A first finger on the rim and a thumb on the foot is a convenient grip for a pot. Any bare patches left by the fingers can be touched up by dabbing with a soft brush full of glaze; avoid any painting action with the brush, which would tend to dislodge glaze already adhering.

Pouring is very suitable for glazing larger and taller pots. The inside is glazed first by pouring in a quantity of glaze from a jug, holding the pot between the hands, and turning it slowly round as the glaze is allowed to run out, so that the whole of the inside is coated with glaze. When glazing bottle shapes, it is often easier to pour in some glaze, cover the mouth with the palm of the left hand, shake the bottle, and then pour out the surplus glaze. When the inside has dried, brush off any glaze which has spilled on to the outside or formed a 'blob' at the mouth. Then fill a jug with the glaze, pick up the pot by the foot with two or three fingers of the left hand, and hold it upside down over a bowl. As the pot is slowly turned with the left hand, flood the outside with glaze from the jug.

This procedure needs a little practice; make some trial runs first, using a jam jar and a jug of water over a sink. The secret lies in co-ordinating the two activities of turning and pouring. Keep the pouring hand steady in one position, and let the glaze fall on to the turning pot – if both are moved, problems will arise. The pouring method is also ideal when a pot is to have different coloured glazes inside and outside. Some touching up of finger marks will be necessary after pouring.

If a pot is too large to be held with one hand, it can be rested across two slats of wood on a bowl placed on the banding-wheel, and the wheel can be spun to rotate the pot.

Well-equipped potteries may possess a spray gun, a compressor, and a booth fitted with an extractor fan. The glaze is sprayed on to the biscuit ware in the same way that paint is sprayed on to car bodies. A banding-wheel inside the booth enables the pot to be turned during coating. Always wear a face mask so that atomised glaze is not inhaled. Spraying is an ideal method of application when glazing biscuit which has been decorated with under-glaze paints or crayons, since it does not disturb the colours. There is one slight problem – layers of glaze must be applied slowly to avoid running, and it is sometimes difficult to apply an even coating.

It is also possible to paint glaze with a mop brush on to soft biscuited articles. Glaze can never be applied with a brush on top of painted biscuit, and the brush method should only be used when none of the other alternatives is feasible.

A NOTE ON CHEMICALS

During the past few years, considerable moves have been made to standardise the naming of chemicals. Unfortunately industry has been slow to adopt some of these, and so chemicals have been referred to in this book by the names used in pottery catalogues. A list of modern names for most of the common chemicals occurring in craft pottery is given in the right hand column of this table. Where there is no change in nomenclature, they have been omitted.

Alumina (Al_2O_3)	Aluminium oxide
Cobalt (black) oxide (Co_3O_4)	Cobalt (II) oxide
Cobalt (grey) oxide (CoO)	Dicobalt (III) oxide
Chromium oxide (Cr_2O_3)	Chromium (III) oxide
Copper (cupric, black) oxide (CuO)	Copper (II) oxide
Copper (cuprous, red) oxide (Cu_2O)	Copper (I) oxide
Iron (ferric, red) oxide (Fe_2O_3)	Iron (III) oxide
Iron (ferrous, black) oxide (FeO)	Iron (II) oxide
Lead oxide (litharge) (PbO)	Lead (II) oxide
Manganese dioxide (MnO_2)	Manganese (IV) oxide
Nickel oxide (NiO)	Nickel (II) oxide
Potash feldspar ($K_2O.Al_2O_3.6SiO_2$)	Aluminium/potassium silicate
Red lead (Pb_3O_4)	Dilead (II) oxide
Silica (SiO_2)	Silicon (IV) oxide
Soda (Na_2O)	Sodium oxide
Soda ash (Na_2CO_3)	Sodium carbonate
Soda feldspar ($Na_2O.Al_2O_3.6SiO_2$)	Aluminium/sodium silicate
Stannic oxide (SnO_2)	Tin (IV) oxide
Stannous oxide (SnO)	Tin (II) oxide

Fig. 271. Tipping out surplus glaze from a pot that has been glazed using the pouring method.

Fig. 272. Pouring glaze over the outside of a jug.

Glossary

Some of the descriptions and definitions given below are necessarily brief, and further information will frequently be found in the text – please consult the index.

Banding-wheel
A revolving turntable on a fixed base, very useful when decorating pots, or when making coiled ware. The turntable is spun by hand.

Bat
Basically a sheet of material on which pots are supported, carried, or dried. Pots can be thrown on removable bats placed on the wheel-head.

Biscuit
Unglazed ware, the result of the first firing.

Biscuit-firing
The first firing. A pot may be decorated before biscuit-firing, but glazing is usually done after this fire.

Body
General term used for any blend of clay and minerals from which pottery is made, e.g. earthenware body.

Casting-slip
Special type of slip used when making pottery with the aid of plaster casts. Ordinary slip cannot be used for this purpose.

Centring
Making the prepared ball of clay run true on the wheel. It is impossible to make a pot unless the clay is perfectly centred.

Cheese wire
Another name for a cutting wire.

Coiled pot
Pot made from narrow rolls of clay, which are coiled one on top of each other, and pressed together to form a pot shape.

Combing
Decoration made by running the fingers or a suitable object through a thin layer of wet slip or glaze on a pot.

Coning
Part of the centring operation. The ball of clay on the wheel-head is allowed to rise up between the hands to form a cone shape; the column is then forced down again with one hand, while the other hand exerts horizontal pressure.

Cottle
An improvised wall erected round a modelled clay shape. Plaster of Paris is poured into the space created; when set, the plaster will have become a mould of the original clay shape.

Cutting wire
A wire for cutting pots from the wheel, or for cutting through lumps of clay when wedging. Handles of cork, wood etc. are necessary at each end, so as not to cut the hands.

Damp box, damp cupboard
A cool, airtight box or cupboard respectively, in which pots will stay moist. Useful for partly completed clay models, and to prevent pots drying out too quickly and perhaps cracking. Sheets of polythene serve the same purpose.

Depressing
The pressing-down part of the centring operation.

Development
The shape obtained after opening out all the sides of a three-dimensional form. Used as a basis for making slab pottery.

Double casting
A method of making pottery whereby a plaster cast is made of both the inside and outside of the master shape. Slip is poured into the space in between.

Earthenware
Term applied generally to baked clay. More precisely, ware which fires to maturity at a lower temperature than stoneware, but which requires a second (glaze) firing to make it vitreous. The only type of ware that can be produced with any type of kiln, including electric ones.

Flop-over mould
A convex mould for dishes. Known also as a hump mould.

Former
Anything natural or man-made, over which a bendable material can be shaped. The term is common to many crafts, and is correctly used when a material is shaped on it rather than poured into it. For example, if a metalworker bends a rod round a stake, the stake is a former, but if he melts the metal and pours it into a shaped sand mould to achieve the same shape, the technique he is using is moulding and not forming.

Glaze-firing
The second firing, taking place after glaze has been applied to the biscuit.

Grog
Ground-up biscuit, used to make a coarser textured clay body.

Hump mould
Another name for a flop-over mould.

Lawn
The potter's term for a sieve.

Leather-hard
Term used to describe clay that has dried to a firm but still damp consistency. The stage at which it may be safely held, without distortion, for further working.

Luting
Joining-up and modelling together of plastic or leather-hard clay, using slip or water.

Majolica
Decorative techniques involving the painting of metal oxides on to a stanniferous earthenware glaze.

Modelling
Welding together pieces of clay, using fingers or tools, e.g. when making slab or coiled pots.

Modelling tool
Tool used for modelling clay together. A variety of shapes is available.

On-glaze decoration
Decoration applied to ware that has been glaze-fired. A further low firing is then carried out to fix it.

Oxide
Compound of a chemical element with oxygen.

Pinch pot
Pot made by pressing the thumb into a ball of clay, which is then shaped and manipulated into a pot form. Known also as a thumb pot.

Plaster of Paris
A form of gypsum which, when mixed with water, sets solid. Used in pottery for mould-making.

Resist agent
Substance, e.g. wax, used to cover a particular area on a pot surface to prevent it from being coated with glaze, slip etc.

Sgraffito
Form of decoration in which slip or glaze are scratched through to reveal the clay beneath.

Slat
Short length of wood, cut to a pre-determined thickness. Clay for slab pottery is rolled out between pairs of slats, to ensure uniform thickness.

Slip
Clay mixed with water to a liquid consistency. Used as a kind of glue for sticking together pieces of plastic or leather-hard clay. Coloured slip can be made up and used in the same way as glaze, to decorate pottery surfaces.

Slip trailer
Device literally for trailing slip on to surfaces, to achieve decorative effects.

Stilt
Three-armed support, used in the kiln for holding pieces that have been glazed underneath – these would otherwise stick to the kiln. The stilt can subsequently be broken off the glazed piece.

Thumb pot
Another name for a pinch pot.

Trailing
Decoration created by pouring glaze or slip in a controlled way through a nozzle on to a pottery surface.

Turning
Tidying-up a thrown pot on the wheel, using a special turning tool. Usually done on leather-hard pots.

Under-glaze decoration
Decoration using pigments or raw oxides, applied before glazing.

Wad-box
Device for extruding coils of clay for making coiled pots or handles. The diameter of the coils can be altered by using different dies.

Wedging
Mixing clay by hand, to make a firm, even consistency, free of air bubbles and impurities.

Index